DEDICATION

To the Children of the World, especially

My grandchildren Benjamin and Robyn in England

My little friend Nicole Stacy in New Mexico

My adopted grandchildren Anouk and Tiah Rosine Coxon in Canada, and Allison and Hilary Pospisil in Iowa, U.S.A.

May they all be given the guidance needed to realise their true potential in a world of peace and harmony.

ACKNOWLEDGEMENTS

To all those people who have helped and guided me in my lifetime, particularly:

My parents for their love,

My children Stephen and Alison and their father, Peter, for their patience and support in my gymnastic days,

My pupils who taught me patience, love and understanding.

My colleagues in the gymnastic world for their stimulation.

My publishers past and present for their belief.

My two brothers and my friends for tolerating an "odd ball".

My friends Joan Benesh in England and Alastair and Helen Morison in Scotland for their ongoing support.

My overseas friends, Steven Stacy and Ray and Lois Larson in New Mexico; Robert and Lina Coxon, Francine Jarry and David Fiske in Canada; Larry and Patricia Kennedy; Ray and Lois Hinkley and Ed and Victoria Pospisil in Iowa, for their love, support, food and shelter when I was on my travels.

The Universe for the many gifts and challenges with which it has presented me.

Thank you all, from my heart.

TOTAL AWARENESS

BY

JEAN HONEYMAN

YOUR WHOLISTIC GUIDE TO PEAK PERFORMANCE

Total Awareness - Your Wholistic guide to Peak Performance

First published 1996 by The Chalice of Trust

Copyright ©1996 by Jean Honeyman

The Chalice of Trust
7 Hothfield Court, Appleby-in-Westmorland, Cumbria CA16 6JD England
+44 (0) 17683 - 53016

Printed by Reeds Ltd
Southend Road, Penrith, Cumbria CA11 8JH
+44 (0) 1768 - 864214

Photography by John Baxter
7 Bridge Street, Appleby-in-Westmorland, Cumbria CA16 6QH
+44 (0) 17683 - 52347

Cover photograph: Andrew Beaumont

Cover
The author enjoying Peak Performance with her grandson, Benjamin

ISBN 0 9527930 0 8

Leotards by: Carita House
Stapeley, Nantwich, Cheshire CW5 7LJ
Tel 01270 627722

THANK YOU

To the photographic model for my book

ALLISON SUMNER

Allison was my pupil for 7 years during which time she was a gymnastics champion many times.   She retired from competitive gymnastics in 1986 but by this time had represented her country as a Senior International in Belgium in 1985 and also in Nice at the World Student Games and in 1986 at the European Championships in Florence.

She epitomises the dream I have for all children that somewhere at sometime they will find someone to inspire and guide them so that they may all, like Allison, realise and fulfil their true potential.

Thank you Allison for those years of hard work and dedication and the joy it brought to me and to many others.

JEAN HONEYMAN

Jean Honeyman was born on 12th April 1939 in Eston, Yorkshire, England. Her early training was for the theatre and for ten years she studied Classical Ballet with the Royal Academy. She later studied Physical Education, specialising in Dance and Gymnastics and received her teachers qualification from the University of Sheffield.

For fifteen years she taught in schools, colleges and universities and in 1976 became free lance and worked with the British Gymnastics Squads and the Welsh Ice Skating Squad as their Dance teacher and Choreographer.

During this time she wrote and had published three books and two training cassettes on Dance, Gymnastics and Choreography.

She was the Founder-Director of three different private schools for Theatre Arts, Rhythmic Gymnastics and Health and Fitness.

In 1987 her 40 years of involvement with physical expression ended when an injury to her spine and subsequent back surgery curtailed her career. To facilitate her recovery she turned to alternative medicine and natural healing methods and a profound spiritual experience changed her pathway in life.

She spent several years living in Spain and travelled through New Mexico, Colorado and Arizona to connect with indigenous cultures.

She now writes, narrates and produces talking books on spiritual awareness.

In 1995 she was the United Kingdom guest speaker at the International Institute of Integral Human Sciences Conference in Montreal, Canada and this led to her being at Iowa, USA, in 1996 for the Global Reunion which brought together cultures from different parts of the world in peace and harmony.

She is currently based in the Lake District in England but travels extensively with her spiritual awareness work speaking to adult groups and also to children in schools and teachers in training.

She has brought together her life time involvement in physical pursuits with her spiritual awareness to create a programme called Total Awareness which helps individuals to look at themselves and their lives as a "whole" and to balance their physical, mental, emotional and spiritual aspects resulting in peace and harmony in their lives.

She is also a Reiki Master and incorporates this into her work.

Her vision is to see centres around the world where adults and children can come to realise their full creative, physical and spiritual expression, by achieving Total Awareness in their lives.

She can be contacted at

The Chalice of Trust
7 Hothfield Court, Appleby in Westmorland
Cumbria CA16 6JD England.
Tel. +44 (0)1768 353016

CONTENTS

PART 2 – continued

PART 3

INTRODUCTION

In retrospect most of us can pin-point a turning point in our lives which seemingly alters our predicted course.

For me this happened in 1987 when an injury to my spine brought to an end a forty year involvement in Classical Ballet, Gymnastics and Ice Skating Choreography.

These things were my life.

From the age of eight years I had immersed myself in a world of music, movement and achievement where the joy of performance went hand in hand with the constant search for physical excellence and where pain and pleasure were equally evident.

It was a logical progression to want to share this joy with others and for over thirty years it was my greatest pleasure to be trusted with the physical development of young children in these areas of creative expression.

Although technically well trained in all my work and with a sound academic background in anatomy and physiology I was also an innovator and I realise now that most of my work at that time was intuitive. I tuned in with the needs of my pupils on an inner level and it was this and my genuine love for them as individuals which brought about our combined success.

In1987 after major back surgery I was unable to walk or move from the waist and could have given up on life as all the things I loved to do were no longer available to me. Inwardly I knew that as one door was closing another was opening and I was being guided in a new direction.

The topics which, until that time, had interested me in a fringe way were now the things to which I would turn for strength and support.

The door to natural healing had opened and presented itself.

Throughout my own lifetime and that of those around me I have experienced miracles in healing and always these have been the result of faith and natural methods.

I define a miracle as

"An unexplainable happening which defies accepted belief or understanding"

and in the course of this book I will mention such happenings when the combination of faith and natural healing methods brought about miraculous cures.

It is my earnest wish that the simplicity of this book which is based upon personal experience will be easy and enjoyable reading and will be the catalyst which encourages you, the reader, to seek further knowledge from the numerous and detailed books which are available and which are written by experts in their own field of knowledge.

It has been my pleasure to meet some of them and to be inspired by their knowledge and dedication.

I sincerely hope that this simple guide to "Total Awareness" will open doors for you all and that you all will experience the joy and exuberance of living life to the full - the holistic way.

PART 1

KNOWING YOURSELF

If we are to achieve success in any part of our lives it is important that we know ourselves and live our lives according to our personal needs.

This need not be selfish.

Without self love and self care we can not hope to help others.

To this end it is vital that we teach our children self help.

To let them know that they have the power to help themselves in every aspect of their lives.

In a search to be good parents and teachers we tend to take away the child's power by exercising control as opposed to guidance.

It has happened to us all and as a result we live restricted lives.

Behind this exercising of control is fear for we are fearful of many things and almost always these fears are not of our own making but are ones which have been passed on to us.

It is not easy to break old behaviour and belief patterns but it has to be done particularly if our lives are being restricted by them.

To this end I would urge all parents and teachers of young children to observe their children as individuals and to closely tune in to their inner needs and to adapt their routines accordingly.

No two children are alike and what is suitable for one is not suitable for another.

It is important not to stereotype our children. More than anything they need to express who they truly are and this expression will take many forms.

One of our greatest mistakes as parents and teachers is to assume that our children have the same likes and dislikes as we do, but how wrong can we be?

So often children are directed into channels to please the parents and teachers rather than to satisfy a creative urge in the child.

Almost invariably, without a natural "feel" for a subject a child will struggle and with the struggle comes pressure which leads to stress and what should be a pleasurable experience becomes an unpleasant one. As the struggles between adult and child continue, fear and control creep in and from then onwards everything is negative.

Great time and patience should be spent on finding the "inner child" which is not difficult, for children, if they are **happy** always express the inner child. The secret then is to allow the child to develop in his or her own way with guidance rather than control from the adults. It may not be the parents' or teachers' way but who is to say that they are correct.

Only the child really knows its true self.

Only the soul of that child knows its true journey.

We can accrue a lot of Karma by **interfering** with the pathway of another.

All parents and teachers act out of belief that what they are doing is correct. No one sets out deliberately to adversely affect another's life, but yet we do.

Adults act as a result of the beliefs they have been taught.

These may be the result of over protective and controlling belief systems which have been handed down to them from their parents and teachers. A lot of the time they are **outmoded** belief systems. They have no place in the **present.**

This moment is the only moment which is important.

This child is the only child which is important.

What happened in the past is not important.

The situations and the children were different.

Even the time was different and times change.

Without interception at some stage patterning can repeat itself for generations.

We do not have to look far in our present society to see instances of this.

However, we are now entering a time of great change when it will be possible to break old patterns and provide for ourselves and our children a more balanced world.

What is needed is the courage to express ourselves as we "feel" best, even if it is not in the accepted way and to encourage our children and pupils to do the same.

Throughout our lives we have been **controlled** by governments, churches, banks and insurance companies, pharmaceutical groups, oil companies and so on. It pays them to keep us controlled. The more we can be kept in **fear** the more we can be controlled.

It would not be to the advantage of any of the above organisations for us to **take our power back into our own hands.**

They create situations which create fear.

We respond to that fear and we are victims.

If we were to **trust** all people we could forget banking our money.

If we only had what we needed in a financial way, there would be no need for banks as we would use our resources as and when we needed them.

If we **trusted** and had **faith** that we are protected, guided and provided for from another realm which is our Creator we would break the pattern of **fear** which is ultimately behind our **dependence** on the above organisations.

Consider seriously why we need all of the above organisations and it ultimately comes back to fear and only fearful people can be controlled.

I do not believe that society would run amok without these things.

We are all divine beings at our core.

The fact that some demonstrate this and others do not does not mean that **all** people lack the potential.

There is **good** in everyone but generations of **fear** and **control** have stifled its expression.

We all have a **shadow side** and even this has to be expressed and guided.

To truly know who we are requires an understanding of all the aspects which are a part of us.

We need to balance the physical, mental, emotional and spiritual parts which make the "whole" person which is from where the term "holistic" is derived.

Throughout the course of this book we will examine all these areas for only by so doing will we acknowledge the whole person.

To achieve Total Awareness in our lives we must take the responsibility of examining our lives from all these angles so that we can bring our lives into balance again for it is only the **out of balance** body which shows **dis ease** which manifests itself in a physical form called disease.

For this reason we will begin at the beginning with the **non physical** aspects of our being which, if left unattended, will seriously affect our well being.

In this connection I would recommend the Louise Hay books *"You can heal your Life"* and *"Heal your Body"*.

Louise Hay is one of many writers who have cured themselves of terminal illness by attending to the **mind** as well as the body.

The suggested reading at the end of this book gives a comprehensive list of other authors whose personal experiences and publications are inspirational.

I encourage all my readers to research all of these.

They are written from the heart with a wealth of practical experience which can only stimulate and aid our personal search for peak performance in our lives.

Without exception all of these people took their lives into their own hands.

They took back their power and through **self belief** and **self love** they turned their lives around.

Self love is not selfish.
It does not mean being indulgent in one's self, it means **respecting** and **honouring the wonderful creation we are.**

We have the power to heal ourselves. It is our birthright.

THE POWER OF THE MIND

THOUGHTS ARE THINGS

The mind is the most powerful thing we have in the prevention of disease.

Thoughts are things and what we think we ultimately bring to us.

If we constantly think good health and positively believe that it is our birthright and available to us at all times, it will be so.

In our inner search for understanding we must be prepared to look at the **shadow side** of ourselves.

Our shadow side is negative and often overshadows the positive, **light** part of us which must be kept to the fore if we are to achieve permanent good health.

We need to be very honest in this personal examination and when we are generally "out of sorts" or drawing into our lives minor health problems we must stop and take a close look at what is negative in our lives and deal with this as well as treating the complaint.

This is basically the concept behind **Homeopathic** medicine.

Most people know that Homeopathic medicine treats with natural substances, but what many people do not realise is that the true Homeopathic doctor will begin by asking many questions about the person which may seem totally unrelated to the illness.

He or she may even say "Tell me about yourself".

It is the cause of the illness which needs to be treated and the cause is usually within the person.

Thus the Homeopathic practitioner is treating the Mind as well as the body.

At a conscious level it is doubtful that anyone would want to bring on an illness, but at a sub conscious level the inner person may not be as balanced as the outer person suggests.

A lonely, unhappy or fearful person may be seeking the comfort from the extra attention even a minor illness brings.

This does not mean that they are hypochondriacs but that they are going through a state of imbalance, probably on an emotional level when it is comforting for the emotional body to have the extra loving attention of caring people.

We have all done this at some time in our lives, particularly as children when we have "play acted" a complaint to have more attention or to get out of something we did not want to do.

Sometimes the play acting can be so good that the symptoms actually manifest themselves.

The body gives us what we ask from it.

The Monday morning tummy ache is very real to a child who does not want to go to school but rather than treating the tummy ache it would be more advisable to enquire into the reason for not wanting to go to school. An unhappy, fearful child will continue to manifest illness to avoid facing the issue.

Many childhood complaints can be traced to emotional sources.

The child with breathing problems is often the one who at a psychological level feels that there is no space to breathe in his or her life.

Maybe this child is from a very busy home where both parents are working and there is a necessity for a very demanding routine.

Perhaps the child is always being rushed from place to place to fit in with this routine or maybe both parents are hasty people.

Whatever the cause this child will feel there is no time or space to breathe.

Often they will manifest their breathing difficulties when it is most inconvenient for the parents, i.e. their most stressful times and the circle is established.

Stress leads to stress.

Stress leads to fear.

Fear leads to another breathing disorder.

It is interesting how chest problems have increased in children in recent times when young families are put under pressure to work and have careers.

The air pollution is blamed for most of this but one wonders.

Even when both parents are not working but where there is stress, there is often a child with asthma or a breathing problem in the family.

When there is insecurity in the home a child will often manifest a breathing problem because of fear. He or she is frightened to the extent that he or she is also frightened to breathe.

A child will hold on to its breath as a form of anticipation.

A fear of what is to come next.

Chest problems are not the only complaint to manifest in this way.

A child will often hold on to its water and develop kidney problems.

Bed wetting is a perfect example.

The child holds on to its water when it has conscious control but when it is asleep and thus relaxed it wets its bed.

Behind most bed wetting is apprehension or fear.

Thus we have a great responsibility to our children to get our own act together for disturbances and imbalances in our own lives will affect, not only our well being, but that of those around us. We do not have to look far to see a family who seemingly stay clear of illness and another which is constantly plagued by it.

Common sense should tell those concerned that it is not natural for whole families to be constantly ill.

There is an underlying reason for this which is not physical but has a mental or emotional cause.

We can not blame heredity.

The past is the past.

Perhaps we would be wiser to look at the "family behaviour patterns" rather than to blame genetics.

We inherit "patterning" only if we choose to do so.

The surest way that we can stay clear of illness is

to think positive and to be happy.

Of these, thinking positive can be cultivated.

It is easy to be drawn into negativity when surrounded by negative people and situations.

Thus the saying, "stay away from negative people" is a valid one.

It is impossible to change someone who does not want to be changed. It is therefore best to keep away from these negative people and situations.

Accept responsibility for your own life and by being positive you will attract positive people into your life.

Like attracts like.

If you attracted negativity into your life ask yourself what was negative about you at the time.

Like attracts like.

Somewhere on your shadow side you attracted negativity in.

It is, therefore, no benefit to blame anyone else for your problems.

Our present situations are our own making. Perhaps not consciously, but on an unconscious level, by letting our shadow side dominate.

I can speak from a personal level on this account.

There was a short period in my life after the break up of my first marriage when I was very fearful and thus very negative. At forty years of age I was alone in the world with children to support. The responsibility of this worried me and worry is negative.

I worried that I might not remain healthy.
I worried that I might not be able to support them.
I worried most of the time.
Worry does not change anything. It merely magnifies it.

In the first six months of this time of being alone **all the things about which I worried happened.**

I was burned in a house fire.

My daughter was thrown from her pony and ended up in hospital with suspected head injuries.

My home was broken into twice.

The things I feared I might lose, I lost.

I was physically attacked.

I was injured in the gym where I worked and could not work

Every single thing **I feared** I invited into my life.

It took all of these experiences to show me that negativity breeds negativity and that to worry about situations only magnifies them more.,

On a physical level I manifested "unusual cells" on a cervical smear test and ended up in hospital for a biopsy and surgery.

In retrospect I see that I invited this cancer scare into my life too.

I was frightened and alone.

In all this time I was separated from other people but most of all from my Creator.

I never once asked for help.

Why do we separate ourselves from the Source of all things when we only have to ask for help and it will be given?

Ask and ye shall receive.

We can all go through negative phases in our lives but it is important to realise the on-going effects of the same and to break the patterning.

Fortunately for me I did not allow the negativity into my work and by keeping positive in this area was able to let the **light** outshine the **dark.**

What it did teach me was how we can become

the victim of our own thoughts.

To become a victim of our own thoughts is more negative than becoming a victim of the thoughts and situations of others.

At least we can change our thoughts.

Energy follows thought and what we think will ultimately present itself.

This is a universal law.

It is our responsibility to ourselves if we are to achieve Total Awareness to only

think positive thoughts,

visualise only what is good in life and allow it to come in.

Never say die.

I mean this in its strict sense but also in its metaphorical sense of never giving up which is achieved by keeping the mind involved with positive thoughts.

When I was 22 years old and only a week before my wedding my mother was diagnosed as having terminal cancer.

After an exploratory operation the extent of the cancer was so great that they stitched her up again, gave her radium treatment and told my father that at the most she had 6 weeks to live.

They did not tell my mother or myself this.

As far as we were concerned she had received an operation to remove her cancerous growth and that this and the radium had cured her.

She and I chose to believe this.

It was a psychological ploy on the part of my father and the medical team.

There was little point in saying anything else for she was literally riddled with the disease in several major organs.

That she and I had something in which to believe was the tool to help her through a very difficult time.

She had already turned to a natural died of **fruit, vegetables** and **salad** and was drinking masses of **water.**

This she had done **intuitively.**

However, she now had a **goal.**

She wanted to see her grandchildren.

Miraculously, although nothing had changed in her cancer she began to regain her strength.

She was only a tiny person, barely 5 feet tall, and she had always been very slim. So slim that she had never had a bust and one of her dreams had been to have more curves.

She developed them.

Her dream became a reality.

In every aspect of her life she was re-born because that is what she wanted and what she believed was possible.

My own innocence as to the real truth gave her added support for she knew I would not have lied to her and my knowledge of anatomy and physiology could always come up with an explanation for a new pain or discomfort.

In our ignorance to the truth we could both create our own belief and this, together with her natural diet, her desire to live and her "never say die" attitude gave her a life extension of 7 years!

She did live to see her grandchildren, three of them, and it was joyous to see her happiness.

The word "die" had not been part of her vocabulary or thoughts and she did not die until the right time for her.

She proved beyond all shadow of doubt that the "never say die" attitude can work but most of all she showed her family and the medical profession that miracles do happen.

VISUALISATION

Visualisation is a natural progression of positive thinking. We can mentally think positive thoughts but to actually visualise the things we want in our lives gives added power to those thoughts.

This can be experienced at all levels and in all situations.

TO CURE EXISTING HEALTH CONDITIONS

imagine any visualisation or picture image that is appropriate to you and your situation.

If you have a lump somewhere use the power of the mind and the imagination to see that lump being melted, swept, blown, or vacuumed away.

Try not to make the procedure a violent one but see it **easily and without effort** being removed.

The cells of the body all have intelligence, not only the brain cells.

All the body feels the **intent** of the person.

The intent must be loving and beneficial to the body and to the person as a whole.

Ask the body's permission to intervene on its behalf.

Affirm that you do what you have to do to enable the body to regain its balance and wholeness.

The cells of the body do hear and understand.

They have both intelligence and memory.

They also know when they are being loved and respected and when they are being abused.

A healthy body is one which is loved and respected and it responds accordingly.

As **energy follows thought** so the cells of the body respond with what they feel the owner of the body wants.

If the individual is filling the body with toxins such as coffee, tea, alcohol and tobacco the body will become toxic and slow down.

It assumes that this is what the individual wants and it gives him or her what they want.

Alternatively if the body is fed clean wholesome food and drinks it will respond with more energy and vitality.

It knows when it is cherished and behaves accordingly.

It gives its owner good health.

The greatest gift we can give our children is the knowledge of how to care for the body and to provide them with the example, not only with nutrition but with attention to our thoughts and attitudes.

Children spend the vast proportion of their lives imitating what they see around them.

They can not be blamed for disorder in their lives if the adults around them are disorganised in their thoughts and behaviour.

VISUALISATION TO CHANGE SITUATIONS

Visualisation can also be used to change existing situations particularly **relationships.**

If there are situations in your life that are causing concern **change them** with visualisation.

See the situation in your mind in a more favourable light.

Create an imaginary picture which is happy and loving.

Consciously bathe the people concerned in this happy and loving light, surround them with the colour **pink** and let the situation go with **love.**

Maintain this pleasant feeling whenever you think of the person or situation.

Sometimes if there are situations between people which can not be resolved it could be that these are not a product of this life but of a previous one.

In this case it is advisable to see the people concerned joined by a cord and then to mentally cut the cord and verbally send the person on his or her way with love.

I know from personal experience that this is possible and can have profoundly good results.

In less dramatic situations it is possible to change something as it is happening.

I remember doing this on a recent train journey when the people in my compartment and myself were all feeling ill at ease by the foul language and aggressive behavior of a drunk.

It went on for some time with no respite when I decided that for my own good and the highest good of everyone in the compartment I would visualise the drunk asleep and not troubling anyone.

He obliged us all by promptly falling to sleep.

It is important when visualising to only visualise what is **in your own highest good and the highest good of all,** otherwise this would be inappropriate intervention on your part.

We are only responsible for our own journey in life and must not interfere in the journey of others, the only exception to this being when we willingly accept responsibility for those who can not care for themselves, i.e. the sick, elderly, young children and animals.

VISUALISATION TO CHANGE YOUR LIFE STYLE

Visualisation can help to change your life style.

Remember that energy follows thought and if you constantly see yourself as a **victim** then this is what you will invite into your life.

Visualise yourself with all the things you desire in life which are **to your highest good.**

If it is for your highest good and for the highest good of those around you it will happen.

Be sure also that it is with the **purest and highest intent.**

To want things because another has them may not be to your highest good and may only serve to feed the shadow side's envy and greed.

This would be taking a backward step in your spiritual development.

Always question your intent in everything you do.

If it is coming from love for your self and for others it will have the loving results of caring, gratitude and compassion from which all positive things flow.

None of us likes to think we have a shadow side but we do and it is important that any visualisation we do is not coming from this side.

Visualisation is a very positive tool if used with pure intent and love.

I firmly believe that it is a technique we should teach our children.

In an unconscious way they do it when they day dream but this habit is one adults try to break for them as being time wasting.

We have all been told to stop day dreaming at some time in our lives.

In the child's own intuitive way he or she is trying to change a situation.

Only when a child is constantly day dreaming should we enquire into the reason for so doing.

Invariably it will be that the present situation is one from which he or she wants to escape.

Day dreams are good if they are accompanied by action.

The child who spends a lot of time alone with his or her own thoughts but then transfers these thoughts into action is being productive.

By and large children are not encouraged to develop the art of **self expression** in its many forms and sadly in many schools today the subjects which are being taken out of the curriculum are the **expressive** ones.

To be unable to express one's self in whatever way leads to blockages of energy and this ultimately leads to illness.

Great attempts should be made to bring creative expression back into our schools.

Without it we are stifling the spiritual growth of our children.

FEELINGS ARE THINGS

In the same way as thoughts are things and can take on a physical form, so too can our feelings.

It is now believed that there are only **two** emotions, **fear** and **love,** and that from fear come all the negative emotions and that from love come all the positive ones.

From this concept it is safe to assume that if we could stay in a state of love at all times towards ourselves and others we would remain positive and with self love and love for others we would remain illness free. This is a strong assumption but it is well grounded in fact.

The feelings we show which are as a result of love, i.e. compassion, caring, warmth, understanding and happiness can not fail to promote good health.
The cells of the body are bathed in warmth, love and positivity.

They respond accordingly.

It is when we slip into negativity in the form of fear that the negative side of our shadow self takes over and we encounter worry, suspicion, anger, jealousy, greed and so on.

When locked into this feeling mode we can not hope to be well.

The body responds with the negativity we are expecting of it and subsequent health problems result.

I have a good friend who recently underwent surgery for breast cancer.

Her immediate reaction to finding she had cancer was "Why me?" but after much inward searching which it was painful for her to do, she now admits that there were areas of her life where she had not forgiven those who had hurt her and that she was carrying grudges.

There were areas too where she realises now that she had felt inadequate and unloved when, as the response from people showed when she was ill, she was **very loved.**

All these thoughts were of her own making.

Happily with her new self respect she is making a good recovery.

There are many authors today who have made detailed studies of this with quite alarming results.

It has been shown by numerous studies how certain illnesses occur when specific personality traits are present.

In general it has been noted that heart patients are angry people or in work situations which are stressful or anger prone. The anger need not be their own, for to be among angry people often results in being drawn into their anger and thus upsetting your own balance.

Arthritic people are often critical of themselves and others with high demands of performance and perfection.

Cancer patients are often resentful about some aspect of their lives and have kept their resentful feelings inside. Often this resentment is a result of their own feelings of inadequacy and lack of self worth which often is a product of their **own thinking,** which is imagined rather than actual.

In my mother's case she felt inadequate because of her height. She was only 4 feet 11 inches and often said how inadequate she felt because people always seemed to be looking down on her.

She also was my father's second wife. His first wife had died when she was very young. She often said that she wished that she had been his first and only wife for this also made her feel second best.

She also found it very hard to accept my half sister as her own and this also led to difficulties particularly in later years when my half sister and father spent time together in pursuits my mother did not follow. The rejection feelings came up for her and these were of her own making.

On close inspection there were many areas in my mother's life about which she was resentful although to all intents and purposes she had the outward expression of a devoted wife and mother and a warm, loving person.

She was all of these things but her shadow side was responsible for creating situations which really did not exist.

I am grateful to her for showing me through her experiences what I need to avoid.

For this reason if we are unfortunate enough to develop an illness we must examine our shadow side and see what it is about ourselves which we do not like which is taking over.

With truth and honesty it is possible to find the emotional or mental cause.

Temporarily it is unpleasant to face the shadow side of which we are not proud but face it we must, if we are to switch back into positivity and Total Awareness .

From this we can see how our mental and emotional attitudes can affect our health and well being and that by moving out of negativity in both these areas we can positively change the way our bodies respond.

In this section we have seen how the body gives us what it thinks we want in response to the mental and emotional messages we put out.

In the next section we will see how this is equally true in our physical body type.

DIET

A great deal has been written in recent times as to what we should or should not eat. Emphasis seems to be placed upon what is harmful to us, leaving people confused and even frightened by latest findings.

It is my earnest belief **that the body knows what is best for it intuitively** and left to its own devices will guide us into what we should eat.

This is true only if we are in a balanced state, mentally, physically and emotionally, but if we are not, then the body can start to crave foods to rectify the imbalance.

Eating disorders like anorexia and bulimia usually stem from psychological disorders where the person eats or does not eat in direct response to messages from the emotions as well as the brain.

The body does guide us well but frequently we do not listen to it.

We have warnings when something is not right but we choose to switch off to the real reason for weight gain or an eating disorder.

Throughout my life I have treated my body with respect and it has served me very well. It was my "expressive tool", my livelihood and therefore a valuable possession. Over the years it has been necessary to adapt my diet as my life style and exercise changed but it is basically the same.

I regard it a blessing to have grown up during the war so that the junk foods of today were not available to us.

As children we did not know the existence of sweets, crisps, biscuits and cakes. Such things were rationed. In the main the people born in the 30's did have a basically healthy diet.

Present day children would benefit from "rationing" of junk foods.

Most foods are safe if eaten in moderation but today's society does not know moderation. The supermarket trolleys at the checkouts are evidence of this.

Most junk foods are high in sugar, salt and preservatives and are not good for the body in large amounts.
Studies show without doubt that colouring is harmful to some children, causing them to become hyper-active.

If encouraged to do so children will eat more beneficial foods but they need to learn by example.

So often we see parents exerting a "do as I say" policy rather than a policy of "do as I do". Our children are mirror images of ourselves.

It is saddening to see overweight parents rearing overweight children.

Personal example is the only answer and it should be all around the child not only in the home. Schools have their part to play.

The young can get away with mis-matches in the foods they put together for their digestion is as yet not under strain, but older people need to pay closer regard to **food combining** which is the order in which foods should be eaten and the way they should be combined.

It is a method of eating which results in the body effectively using the food so that none is stored and the resulting energy is greater.

Our bodies are effectively food combustion chambers and the secret of peak performance is to find which combinations of food are most effectively used by the body.

There are many good books published on food combining but the following information will act as a guide and a brief resumé.

FOOD COMBINING

The essential thing to remember in the correct combining of food is to separate the complex carbohydrates, i.e.

Bread, Potatoes, Rice from the **Proteins.**

This means that it would not be sensible combining to put bread, potatoes or rice with meat, fish, cheese or eggs.

Therefore

Meat   **Rice**

Fish
              with   **Potatoes**   **NO.**
Cheese

Eggs   **Bread**

The reason for this is that the stomach has two digestive enzymes which work independently on the proteins and the carbohydrates. They can not work at the same time. Preference will be given to the digestion of the protein and as a result the carbohydrates are not digested and are stored.

The correct combination would be

Meat   **Vegetables**

Fish
              with   **and/ or**   **YES.**
Cheese

Eggs   **Salad**

The question then is how to include complex carbohydrates into the diet without mis-matching and the answer is to keep the complex carbohydrates with other carbohydrates. For example:

Potatoes   **Vegetables**

Bread   **with**   **and/or**

Rice   **Salad**

It can be seen that vegetables and salad combine with anything.

When re-educating the digestive system in this way it is difficult at first to break old habits but changes do have to be made.

For example

Spaghetti Bolognaise with Meat sauce becomes

Spaghetti Bolognaise with Vegetable sauce

Curried dishes such as

Chicken curry with rice becomes

Vegetable curry with rice.

Sandwiches are more difficult for it is traditional to have protein fillings in sandwiches. All meat, fish, eggs and cheese must be left out which only leaves salad and banana.

It can be done but just requires a little more thought.

FRUIT

It is advisable to only eat fruit on its own and to do this early in the day, preferably at breakfast.

It is advisable to eat fruits alone and not mix them with other fruits as they all have different enzyme actions.

If fruit is not substantial enough for breakfast it can be eaten throughout the morning leaving half an hour between each piece but leaving one hour between if the fruit type is changed.

Some fruits have stronger enzymatic powers than others. These are:

Apples
Pineapples
Strawberries
Kiwi
Papaya
Water melon

These fruits will help to burn food and cleanse the system.

Grapes are particularly good cleansers of the intestine but like water melon they should be eaten alone.

Breakfast   **Fruit**

Mid Day Meal   **Carbohydrates**

To place the emphasis on carbohydrates at mid day is important as carbohydrates when eaten alone quickly change to sugar in the body and give instant energy when it is most needed.

Some examples would be:

Vegetable soup with bread
Salad with baked potatoes
Vegetables with rice
Salad sandwiches

Evening Meal   **Protein**

The earlier the evening meal the more beneficial to the body.

It is good sense not to eat after 5 p.m. as to eat later puts strain on the body when it should be resting.

Evenings are the best time to include protein because the protein has all night to digest.

This combination would be

Meat

Fish
                with   **Salad and/or vegetables**
Cheese

Eggs

Eating as strictly as given here does not allow a lot of variety but with the help of a good food combining book it is possible to be more flexible and include dairy produce and grains.

In my experience with performers I have found that too much dairy produce produced mucus and often the performers suffered with sinus and chest problems.

In our society great emphasis is placed on young children drinking a lot of milk but often children react to cow's milk and have to use other forms - and other children develop respiratory infections through drinking any sort of milk.

Once again it is very important to study the individual child.

Beverages are another debatable topic for studies show that tea and coffee can be just as toxic to the body as alcohol.

There are decaffeinated teas and coffees now available which are less toxic in their caffeine content but others claim that more chemicals are used in the processing and these can be just as damaging. Thus it would seem appropriate to opt for something else.

There are many herb teas which are available, each with its own health giving properties. Again it is advisable to buy a book on herb teas to benefit fully from all the different types.

A refreshing and stimulating drink which I drink all the time is

Hot water Honey   Lemon   Ginger

The cleansing effect of this is good and it is pleasant.

Hot water on its own is cleansing particularly for the liver and a good habit to form is to take

Two glasses of hot water in the morning
and
Two glasses of hot water at night,

The water should have boiled and cooled slightly.

Over the years when working with ladies' health and fitness groups I have encouraged them to try and include basic food combining into their eating regime and to drink more water, particularly the hot water at night and in the morning.

They rapidly see the difference in their energy levels, weight and skin condition.

Most of the time our bodies are toxic because they are never cleaned out and most of the time the liver is working overtime to rid the body of toxins.

It goes without saying that excess alcohol is very hard work for the liver.

Once again balance and moderation in all things is the most beneficial for the body.

CLEANSING

Whilst considering what we put into the body it is also important to consider how we cleanse it.

The body can become toxic if the elimination from the body is sluggish and irregular and particularly if a high protein diet is being followed or eaten in excessive amounts.

To change to a diet high in fruits, vegetables, salad and grains will result in better elimination but from time to time a cleansing regime will help to keep the body toxin free.

A sluggish tired body is often the sign of a toxic body as is a furred, white coated tongue.

When these things occur it is advisable to drink more water, up to 8 glasses a day and to stop drinking tea and coffee. Substitute these with herb teas or hot water.

In addition to this have one day a week, preferably the same day, to do a body cleanse.

A simple and effective way is to have a **fruit fast** once a week.

This will help to cleanse the body but will also rest the digestive system.

When choosing to fruit fast it is advisable to drink plenty of water.

The cleansing effect of water is miraculous and there have been two occasions in my life when the use of water has prolonged or saved a life.

The first I have already mentioned when my mother took to drinking only water when she had cancer. The second was an incident which happened to me after my back surgery when I was given pain killers which gave me toxaemia.

For three days I was very close to death.

My pulse was 150: my temperature 104; I could not close my mouth as my tongue was so swollen and white;' my body swelled out of all proportion and I had a violent migraine headache accompanied by nausea.

My intuition told me to drink water and for three days and nights I did this. Within three days I had recovered.

In general we do not drink enough clear water in our diet.

6 to 8 glasses a day is a required amount.

Apple Fast

In deciding to follow a fruit fast it is advisable to stick to a single fruit and my favourite one is apples.

The reason for this is that apples are

Inexpensive

Available all year round

Easy to eat

Easy to carry

Apples are very enzymatic and help to burn stored protein and cleanse the body.

They can be eaten as regularly as every half hour.

There is a possibility that they may produce "the runs" but this, after all, is the object of the exercise.

When I was teaching in my own movement studio and teaching a minimum of eight classes a day on the hour, I did not have time to eat standard meals at standard times or have the time to digest the food in between classes.

For this reason my principal diet was apples supplemented by a light evening meal and I kept very fit and active on this simple diet.

Pineapple Diet

Of all the enzymatic fruits pineapple is probably the most effective when it comes to burning stored protein and cleansing the body.

In the book *The Beverley Hills Diet* pineapple plays a very large part in the cleansing regime.

It is an interesting book but it takes fruit cleansing to extremes and before embarking upon a diet such as this it would be a good idea to have already tried a weekly fruit fast.

Strawberry

Kiwi   These are all fasts which use strong enzymatic fruits

Papaya

Grape fast   Grapes clean the intestine but can result in a very loose bowl action if eaten in large mounts.

Water melon fast   These encourage the release of water from the body and are thus diuretic.

Not one of the once a week fruit fasts is harmful to the body and can be very beneficial.

Similar effects can be achieved with a once a week

Vegetable juice fast Again, it is advisable to keep to a single vegetable and my own preference would be

Carrot juice fast   Continue to drink several glasses of water a day as well as the juice. One disadvantage of the vegetable juice fasts, particularly if they are continued for several days, is that they can make the breath very smelly and also lead to gas.

Further reading on these topics appears in the suggested reading.

SPECIAL NEED DIETS   ARTHRITIS

In the discussion of diet so far emphasis has been placed on the need for cleansing the body from time to time and also for the need to include plenty of fresh foods such as fruit, vegetables and salad as the recuperative benefits of these foods are very great.

I have an on-going back injury which sometimes limits my physical ability and capabilities.

Recently I attempted to clear my building site garden of weeds, dig it over and plant it out in four days. The result for the garden was wonderful but the effect on my lower back, neck and hands was devastating.

The pain, swelling and heat was indescribable and it was then that I realised that I had sparked off arthritis, in these vulnerable areas.

By chance, when I most needed it, I came across Giraud Campbell's book *A Doctor's Proven New Home Cure for Arthritis* in a flea market.

I took this home and began to follow the diet suggested and after the first cleansing day felt a significant improvement in the head and neck pain and by the end of the first week was feeling relief in the lower back.

Most of what Giraud Campbell has to say has already been said in this book for although he does not actually recommend food combining the mere fact that he eliminates bread and rice from the diet does mean that the result is a diet of protein combined with **fresh vegetables, salad and fruit.**

He also eliminates tea, coffee, alcohol and any other toxic drinks and advocates fruit juices but not of the acidic variety i.e. orange, lemon or grapefruit.

What was reassuring for me was to know that the diet I had developed for myself was one which would, in fact, with a few small changes, assist in the curing of arthritis.

Giraud Campbell advocates stepping up the supply of **certified milk** to ensure a more ready supply of calcium and as most milk is tampered with in some way now the best possible milk is probably **goat's milk.**

A brief outline of the **arthritis free diet** is given below and a detailed account can be found in Giraud Campbell's book.

Foods to be avoided:
All preserved food
Anything made with flour
Anything frozen
Anything tinned
Coffee, tea, alcohol, soft drinks
Jams, jellies, preserves, sweets, ice cream etc.
Cereals

Foods to be taken:
Fresh vegetables, fruit and salad eaten raw
Certified milk
Cod liver oil
Molasses
Cider Vinegar
Brewer's Yeast
Offal type meats i.e. kidneys, liver, etc.
Fish

Oranges, lemons, grapefruit, pineapple and other acidic fruits should be avoided.

WE ARE WHAT WE EAT

Regardless of what we have been led to believe it is possible to stay the same shape and weight throughout or lives.

The weight may be distributed slightly differently and the body may not have the firmness all over which it had during its youth but there is no reason why it should not remain similar to what it was in its youthful state.

In almost all cases of **excess weight** the most prevalent causes are:

Unbalanced diet

Unhappiness

Lack of self respect

Boredom

Lack of exercise

Loneliness

It will be seen that to take a balanced diet of proteins, fats and carbohydrates and to food combine them will greatly assist in keeping the body weight stable.

If combined with a once a week body cleanse and increased water consumption the body will soon become more energised.

TO BE OR NOT TO BE VEGETARIAN?

It is doubtful that all those people who are vegetarian today came from practising vegetarian families.

Somewhere along the line an individual feels the need to become vegetarian.

Usually this is not something which happens overnight but is when the desire for meat becomes less and less.

If this is the case and it is not a fad to keep up with the trend of the day, the chances are that it is right for the individual for the body does know best.

For my own part I never particularly liked meat and could have functioned without it but at the time of my back surgery when I needed all my energy to get well I stopped eating meat.

It was as if my body made the decision because it had other more demanding uses for the energy.

For the most part I am now a non meat eater.

We can not make hard and fast rules for other people for all people have different needs. Regardless of the ethical situation of killing animals for food it has been suggested that some body types based upon their blood groups do need meat. The 'O' blood groups, both Rhesus Positive and Rhesus Negative, fall into this category.

The difference ethically is how the animals are reared and how they meet their death. Animals which are raised free and have a humane existence do not carry in their meat the bad vibrations of animals raised in bad conditions and slaughtered inhumanely. The meat of animals does carry the vibration of the animal and it is this which is often not acceptable to the human body.

Meat is still, in the West, our most usual form of protein but there are other forms.

Children need protein for body building as do athletes who require more muscle. Without meat some of these people may be short on body building material.

Evidence has come forward to point to the fact that children raised in vegetarian families who have no meat at all in their diet are more likely to develop leukaemia than any other category.

I would be very much inclined to suggest that we all listen to the body on this issue and to allow children to be guided by their likes and dislikes.

On the ethical issues of meat eating what we can do is to lobby for more humane rearing, transportation and slaughter of animals.

The indigenous races honoured the animals they killed.

They first asked permission of the animal and by giving it an honourable death ensured that its spirit left the body.

These concepts are not familiar to our society and they require more understanding of our connection to the universe.

The animals are our brothers and sisters.

Would we slaughter our human brothers and sisters and eat them?

People must decide how best they can come to terms with this issue.

To conclude this section the best advice is to

Listen to the body and to eat those foods which seem best at the time but be sure that any changes in eating habits are not the result of boredom or are a way to substitute for self love and fulfilment.

FEEL THE FEELINGS OR FEED THE FACE?

Earlier in this section I mentioned that in my work I have noticed that with the exception of glandular problems there are three principal causes of weight gain:

Unhappiness

Lack of self respect

Boredom

Loneliness

In each case it can be rectified but it necessitates the inner searching which we are reluctant to do.

Somehow we feel inadequate knowing that we have allowed our emotions or thoughts to bring us to this unhappy situation.

It is not easy to "pick up the tab" for one's own unhappiness but the truth is that situations and people can only make us unhappy **if we allow them to do so.**

Regardless of what is going on around us we must try to maintain our own **self belief** and **positivity,** which is not easy when presented with difficult circumstances.

Unhappiness and lack of self respect often go hand in hand so can be tackled together.

When either situation appears **write down** all the things there are in your life about which you are **grateful.**

The list is very long when you start saying thank-you for all the things we normally take for granted.

Follow this by **writing down** all the things you like about yourself, and there are many if you clear away the immediate hurt.

Put on your positive hat and see yourself as you really are and not as the people, situations and you shadow side would have you believe.

When you are happy, confident and involved the urge to binge on chocolate bars and junk food is not so great.

There are too many exciting things waiting to be done.

A fat body does not want to be a fat body and by eating comfort foods the hurt person is only temporarily soothed.

When the realisation hits the person that they have succumbed yet again, anger results and the person is less happy with herself than before.

It is a vicious circle.

Junk foods only feed the feelings of inadequacy and only you can break the pattern.

Boredom slips into this category very easily and frequently results in haphazard eating patterns.

To avoid boredom **write down** the things you would like to do and **make a start on achieving them** either with visualisation or in a practical way and if you are still bored

exercise the body. There is nothing better to stimulate the brain and invigorate the body than exercising it.

It is possible to feel totally drained from a trying day and within an hour or so to feel re-born and the key factor was **exercise.**

The body is a superb machine and all machines benefit from use.

Exercise the body for

A fit body which is well exercised feels loved and respected.

It responds to exercise and this does not have to be violent, exhausting or technical.

A brisk walk in the fresh air is enough to get the cells singing again.

A Spanish doctor once said of my body condition, "This lady's body makes good music".

I was intrigued by this association but afterwards thought how apt it was for a fit body does "sing". The cells are happy to be alive and they perform with vibrancy.

Too many exercise regimes fail because they are too demanding upon the person in time or effort.

If something is to be beneficial it needs to be regular and a simple, short, less demanding exercise daily is preferable to an exhausting once a week workout.

Exercise should be as easy and frequent as brushing the teeth.

Walking

This is the simplest form of exercise and if done daily for approximately one hour would greatly improve the cardio vascular system and tone up the body.

Within every person's daily routine it must surely be possible to fit in a daily walk.

Swimming

A weekly swim improves the breathing, circulation and stamina.

Flexibility

Exercises of the more gentle Yoga variety will keep joints and muscles supple and also improve the circulation and breathing.

Breathing

Something we all overlook but which is vital to our well being is breathing. Without adequate air we are starved of the oxygen necessary to the body. The old practise of deep breathing in front of an open window was a sensible one. The air may be polluted today but a healthy immune system can cope with it and polluted air is better than no air at all.

MOVEMENT PROGRAMME

An effective movement regime is one which can be done daily without major disruption to normal routine. It should include:

Locomotion   i.e.   **Walking**

Breathing

Flexibility

A very complete exercise regime is Yoga which incorporates all of these things. Thus Yoga combined with a daily walk would be an adequate regime for the body.

In compiling the Movement Programme for this book I have tried to create movements based as closely as possible on the body's natural movement which places emphasis on the spine whose natural movements are to

Bend

Stretch

Twist

I have endeavoured to keep all exercises within the bounds of the untrained person.

On the surface they may seem too simple but I have seen the adverse effects of over training on the body and the destruction caused by unnatural body movements.

Something does not have to be complicated to be effective.

These are the exercises I give to my own body even though there are other more technical ones I could do.

The result, if performed correctly, will be total freedom and flexibility of movement.

When performing this movement programme I would ask that you treat it as a holistic time in your day and that you are aware of the mind, body, spirit as you work.

This is not only a physical time of the day. It is a time which can be very spiritual also.

Purely physical routines exercise the body but they do not nurture the soul and when the soul is joyful the whole being of the person is enriched and nourished.

To this end I would ask that you regard this part of your day as

Moving meditation.

To this end it is important to create an atmosphere which will touch the soul as well as the body.

Preferably find a quiet place in your home and select your favourite classical or inspirational music.

I have my classical favourites but of inspirational music I find the music of Robert Haig Coxon, the Canadian composer, to be ideal.

A soft rug or carpet is preferable to a hard floor for some of the exercises involve rolling on the spine which can cause bruising.

Create a relaxing atmosphere in any other way which pleases you.

To light candles or to have an aromatic oil burning soothes the senses and beautifies the environment.

The body enjoys to be treated as precious, for it is.

A little luxury makes for a more pleasant environment in which to work.

MOVEMENT 1

Breathing

A

B

In back lying, knees bent, feet flat on the floor.

Hands placed across the diaphragm, finger tips touching.

On the in breath allow the abdomen to rise and the ribs to lift and swing outwards. The fingers will move apart.

On the out breath allow the abdomen and ribs to flatten and the fingers to come together again. Repeat as many times as necessary to feel completely relaxed.

When you are breathing in imagine that you are breathing in all that is **good.** When you breathe out imagine that you are breathing out all negativity.

MOVEMENT 2

Breathing

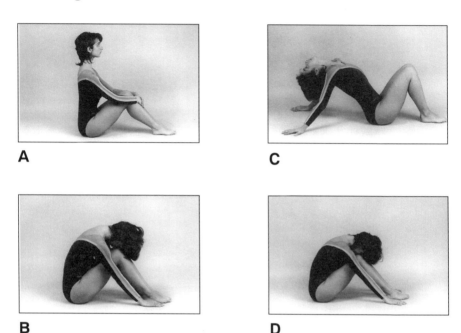

A

C

B

D

In sitting on the floor in upright position, with knees bent feet flat on floor, **Breathe in.**

Breathe out when moving forwards to place the head on the knees. Hands to feet.

Repeat as necessary.

In sitting on the floor, arms extended behind the body and head dropped back (c).

Breathe in then move forwards to the head on to the knees position.

Breathe out in this position.

Keep the lungs empty of air as you move back to the start position

Breathe in at position (a).

Breathe in all that is good and breathe out all that is negative.

Feel the cleansing effect of this on the body.

MOVEMENT 3

Breathing

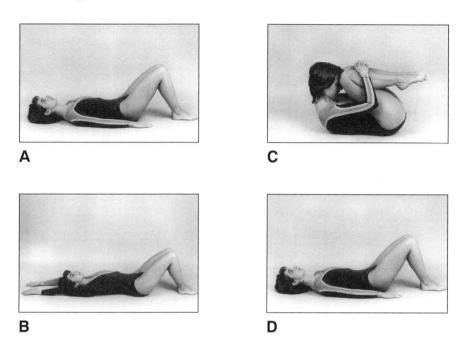

A

C

B

D

In lying with arms by the sides. Knees bent, feet flat on floor.

Breathe in and take the arms over the head - straight.

Breathe out and bring the arms back to the knees, drawing up the knees to touch the head.

Return to the start position with the lungs empty of air.

Breathe in and repeat.

MOVEMENT 4

Rolling

A

B

In back lying roll up on to the shoulders and stay in this position, with knees to the forehead.

Hold as long as possible in this position.

Keep **breathing** and feel the back muscles moving out and in.

Repeat.

MOVEMENT 5

Roll And Fold Combination

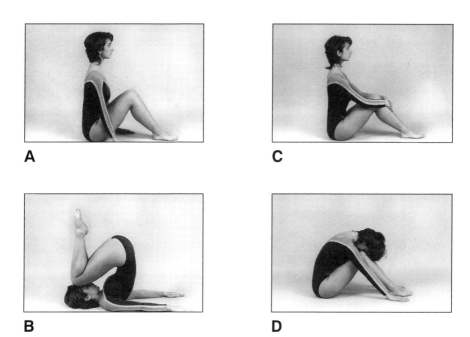

A

C

B

D

From sitting, knees bent, roll back on to shoulders and hold.

Roll forwards up to sitting, to put head on knees.

Repeat as often as required.

When rolling forwards and backwards try to keep the spine rounded, not flat.

It should be a smooth rhythm and sound.

MOVEMENT 6

Stretch And Fold

A

B

C

Begin in a sitting position with knees bent, and allow the knees to stretch keeping the head near to the knees.

Stop if there is pain or tension behind the knees.

Gradually aim to touch the head on the knees keeping the knees straight.

This should be easy and without effort.

It is of no advantage to strain against tight muscles.

Relax with the music, think pleasant thoughts and day by day come closer to touching the head on the knees.

MOVEMENT 7

Roll, Stretch and Fold

A

B

C

Eventually combine the backward roll with the forward stretched fold to give maximum curling and stretching throughout the spine.

Be sure to bend the knees **in** as you roll forward from back lying.

Legs are only straight when supported by the floor.

MOVEMENT 8

Abdominal Toning Combined with Curling and Stretching

A

B

C

From back lying, knees bent, feet flat on floor, bring the arms straight over the head and straighten the knees to come up to sitting.

Forward fold over straight legs.

Come back to sitting, bending the knees and return to back lying.

Repeat as often as desired.

This should be a very smooth, rhythmic exercise performed with effortless ease.

The movement of the arms straight over the head helps to lift the body and the thrusting of the legs from bent to straight prevents back strain.

Remember to **bend** the knees as you come up and return to the floor, otherwise the back will be strained.

MOVEMENT 9

Twisting the Spine

A

B

Sit with one leg straight and the other bent but crossed over the straight one.

Facing forwards

Twist the body to the right and left alternately so that the top of the body is moving in opposition to the hips.

Change legs.

MOVEMENT 10

Twisting and curling the Spine

A

B

In sitting one leg straight and the other leg bent and crossed over the straight leg.

Fold forwards to bring the head down on to the front foot.

Change legs and repeat on the other side.

MOVEMENT 11

Extending the Spine

Lying on the tummy, weight on forearms and elbows bent.

Hands are close to the ears.

Extend the elbows to push the body upright.

Try to get the back at right angles to the seat and legs

Hold as long as possible.

Return to the floor.

MOVEMENT 12

Rounding the Spine

To counteract the extension of the previous movement move into a kneeling position and place the head to the floor with back rounded and seat still in contact with the heels.

Keep sitting on the feet with hands holding on to feet.

MOVEMENT 13

Hip Mobility

In back lying with both knees bent, kick one leg straight above the head and return it to the floor with knee bent.

Repeat with the other leg.

The amount of movement will depend upon the length of the **hamstring muscles.**

Try for ninety degrees above the head and then for more.

MOVEMENT 14

Stretching

A

B

With feet approximately 12 inches apart, bend knees to assume a standing squat position.

Feet are facing straight forwards, not turned out.

Stretch up and swing the arms above the head, fingers clasped and arms straight

Lift the rib cage and extend the spine.

Swing down easily and unlink the hands, letting the arms swing behind the body.

Bend the knees

MOVEMENT 15

Bends and Rises

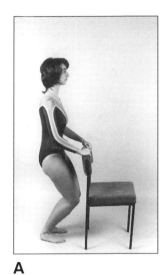 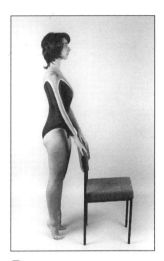

A   **B**

Feet approximately 12 inches apart, facing forwards and straight.

Bend the knees keeping the heels in contact with the floor, seat tucked in and back straight.

Follow this by a rise on to the toes.

Have a support - either hold on to a chair or touch the wall.

Keep the movement slow and smooth.

MOVEMENT 16

Plantar and Dorsieflexion for feet and ankle

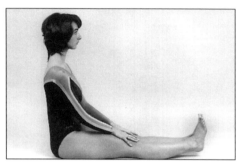

A

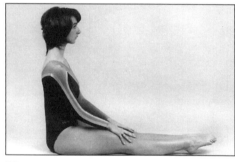

B

In long sitting with legs straight and supported by the floor.

Alternately point the toes down to the floor and then pull them back up to face the ceiling

When this is easily accomplished try to do it with the heels **off** the floor.

This is much harder on the thigh muscles.

Cooling down movements

In standing, gently shake the hands and feet, relax the arms and legs and shake the arms and legs.

Gently shake and wriggle the whole body, particularly the spine.

Perform simple head rolling movements to relax the neck and shoulders.

Swing the arms gently backwards and forwards.
With the music do any free **expressive movements** which feel appropriate to you, and which help you to express yourself in movement.

These simple movements will soon be accomplished and it may then be enjoyable to join other movement classes and extend your movement ability.

LONELINESS

This is a contributory factor to ill health and by taking **walks, going swimming** or attending **gentle exercise classes** it will be possible to combine a healthy interest in movement with some social contact and help overcome the loneliness.

We tend to think we are the only lonely people when we are feeling lonely but there are many people who live alone and feel the same way.

The secret is not to shut yourself away but to get out even if it is only for a walk.

Even if you are not lonely remember that others are and your ready smile and conversation can do a great deal to brighten a lonely person's day.

It may be the only contact they have had with anyone that day.

REST AND RECUPERATION

As well as stimulating the mind and body with a healthy diet, fresh air and exercise it is also important to **rest** the body and mind and give it the chance to recuperate and regenerate. To be active is good but to be over-active is not.

The body and mind need refreshment in the form of relaxation and to enjoy life for enjoyment's sake.

Without relaxation, a change of scene and **humour** life can become too serious.

We have great capacity for joy in our lives but rarely express it to the full in our constant search for achievement.

Laughter makes the world go round and is also a healthy recipe for good health.

Norman Cousins in his book *"Anatomy of an Illness"* gives as the two main contributory factors to his recovery from a terminal illness his ability to keep laughing and large doses of Vitamin C.

We always joked that my mother would die laughing because laughter played a big part in her life.

In her final days the last time she was conscious she had to go back to bed to lie down after laughing so much at a television programme that she hurt.

She did not regain consciousness so came very near to fulfilling our prophesy.

Dr Effie Chow the *Qi Gong* Master advocates four good belly laughs a day and not without cause.

Laughter is the finest medicine and in its expression of joy is a great tonic for a tired body.

Listen to the body and sleep when the body requests it.

Sir Winston Churchill was famous for his **cat naps**.

After a brief respite he could then work for many hours.

Our bodies know what is best.

Listen to them and take frequent rests and naps.

SLEEP

The function of sleep is regarded by most as a time the body can rest and recuperate, and this is so.

The cells of the body are renewing themselves constantly and according to Deepak Chopra we have no need for illness or damaged organs if we work with our bodies as their ability to regenerate is far greater than we know.

Although one aspect of sleep is to allow our bodies to regenerate another important aspect is to allow the sub conscious to come to the surface in the form of **dreams.**

We trap old memories and feelings in the sub conscious and when the control of the conscious is removed these are allowed to surface, to be recognised and expressed.

Everything which enters the sub conscious before sleeping is magnified and it is therefore good policy to rid yourself of negative thoughts before going to sleep otherwise they will magnify.

On the positive side to think positive and be happy before going to sleep will magnify these also.

Academic students have found that the facts put into their brains before sleep do seem to be more easily retained.
Some take this further and have audio tapes playing during sleep so that the facts can enter the sub conscious.

Another function of sleep which is not commonly known is to allow the **soul** to journey independently of the body during the sleeping hours.

The soul is the only part of the body which is everlasting.

It is pure energy and energy in its purest form can not be destroyed.

The body is dense energy and has a limited life span particularly the way we lead our lives today.

At some point the body has to be discarded to allow the soul to return to its origins which are from the **universe** where it will temporarily reside to take stock of the life just accomplished before returning to Earth, through **reincarnation,** to continue with its journey.

The body is merely the vehicle which houses the **soul** and, although important, is secondary in importance to the **soul's journey.**

For this reason it is important to recognise the **soul's journey** and to look to the spiritual aspects of our lives also.

In a simple way the soul does this for us during sleep when it leaves the body and travels to other realms where it experiences that which is necessary to its Earth journey.

Many people can remember this experience particularly those who have had **near death** experiences when they have been aware of leaving their bodies and looking down on their physical self.

This is what happens during sleep and is not something which should be considered disturbing but recognised as being perfectly normal.

THE SPIRITUAL SELF

In following holistic health practises we are always attempting to treat the whole person.

So far we have considered how this can be done from a physical and mental point of view but little mention has been made of the spiritual.

As people who care for ourselves totally and are looking to be whole this can not be overlooked.

Holistic health must embrace the

mind   **body**   **spirit.**

Western societies are not as active in their nurturing of the spirit as are Eastern, Oriental and Indigenous races.

One very obvious difference between these and Western societies is their belief in the **after life,** their joy when it is time to die, and their great respect for the departed spirits who are now in other realms.

In the West our belief in the after life and reincarnation are not encouraged.

Indeed some churches forbid this notion.

The reason for this is quite obvious.

If every person were to believe that this life was only a part of a very long journey and that reincarnation is the means whereby we can work out our life's lessons and grow spiritually there would be no need for the control of the church.

It is not in the interests of the church to have individuals secure and happy on their spiritual pathway.

There is a place in our lives for basic teachings and guidance and this is the role of the church but when it results in control then it takes away the individual's freedom of choice and Earth is a planet of free will and choice.

This was the gift we were given at the Creation and it is a gift we have not used wisely.

Principally because fear and control are a part of our existence.

Without fear and control we could continue our spiritual growth with greater ease.

The most productive thing anyone can do if they are to be more spiritual is to try and eliminate fear and control from their lives.

We may feel we are not fearful and controlling, but we are.

I can look back on my own life when I have reacted out of fear and many times when I have tried to control others.

Guidance is not control

To guide people is unconditional and has no strings attached.

There is freedom of choice on the part of the receiver.

Without conditions the guidance is an act of love and from love comes positivity for love is the most powerful and positive of all energies.

Control is not unconditional.

It relies on rules and is a power game.

The person making the rules exerts the power and the receiver is often in fear of that person or the outcome.

From fear comes negativity which develops into anger, mistrust, envy and greed, which ultimately affect the health.

We do not want to affect the health of those around us by exercising control, particularly our children.

Children respond best to **firm guidance ...**

Firm in so much as it is constant and dependable as opposed to rigid.

Children give adults what is expected of them and if they are **guided lovingly** they will respond in this way.

Children do not come into this world with the intention of being awkward or unruly.

Children **want** to learn.

It is the direction they receive, the love with which they are surrounded and the dedication of those with whom they interact which influence their progress.

It has been my life times work to be with children and it has been **joyous.**

I have learnt from them.
Because I love them and sincerely want to give of my best to them they always respond.

Children are very intuitive.

They are not fooled by pretence.

They see straight to the person and often through him.

On our own spiritual journey it is very important to leave fear and control out of our own lives and not to allow others to influence us in these ways.

Without fear and control we are free to be ourselves and it will be much easier to operate from love.

It is not easy to be yourself in Western society which tries to categorise us all and put us into "boxes".

To be yourself you have to be prepared to be classed as an "odd ball" or a non-conformist which are labels carefully chosen and construed to make us "toe the line". It is a struggle against the odds but that can be a challenge.

There comes a point when by discovering that you are an odd ball you can be fairly sure that you are being an individual.

By being individual you are expressing parts of your true self that are essentially you which are aspects of your spirituality and which are very precious.

You are expressing honesty and truth about who you really are and these qualities go a long way in creating sound relationships and harmonious societies.

A fault of our Western society today is that we have been controlled by governments, churches and other organisations which have not been totally honest with us.

If we are to make changes it can be done at our individual level and to begin to be honest and true to ourselves and others will make waves.

We do not need to keep referring to the scriptures to keep us on our spiritual pathway for if we operate out of love we have all religions expressed within that one word.

It is really as simple as this.

The examples the scriptures give us are helpful but the real message is **Love.**

This is true of all religions and whilst they have a place in society the true religion is the one **within ourselves.**

We must never forget from whence we came and to what we are eternally linked.

We are part of our Creator but we have forgotten this

In our isolation we have thought we were alone but we are never alone or separated from the source of all things.

We are linked by the **universal energy.**

The **Chi, Prana, Holy Spirit,** call it what you may, but we are linked.

We only have to believe this one simple truth and live our lives in **love and our problems disappear.**

We create our own problems and in the main it is because of fear and control at some stage in our lives.

We can change our lives in a twinkling of an eye.

If we feel that we are victims we must change it.

Seek out what is making you feel a victim and refuse to be victimised which is only control.

We do not have to be controlled.

We have freedom of choice.

We can say no, but this takes courage and we do not have courage if we are in fear, but we need not have fear because we are never alone.

We need only ask for **guidance.**

We have a loving **Creator** waiting to be asked but we do not ask.

We struggle on in our isolation and separation and forget that **our greatest strength is our connection to the Creator.**

When considering what the Creator was responsible for creating we should feel very safe.

Prayer is not something we should turn to when we are in a mess.

Prayer should be a daily talk with our Creator, easily and fluently from the heart.

Set prayers have their use if we have nothing else to say but the Creator needs to know our personal requests.

One of the beautiful aspects of Native American Culture is the loving way they talk to Great Spirit.

The Creator is in everything so that every time we talk to the trees or the birds we are talking to the Creator.

The **Creator** is in the plant, animal, mineral and elemental kingdoms and in each and every person.

If we were to recognise this and to interact with all living things as if we were talking or interacting with our Creator then the world would be a very changed place.

It has been a source of great joy to me to visit **New Mexico** and to experience the Native American Culture at first hand.

The simplicity and beauty of their caring for nature and the Universe, their respect for their elders, living and in the spirit world, and their ability to **love** even after all the hardship they have endured is inspirational.

In the West we are quick to put down other races because on an economic level they do not appear as affluent or advanced as we are but how wrong can we be?

Spiritually they are rich indeed and we have a lot to learn from their simplicity.

The world is in turmoil and when the "crunch" comes it will be to the indigenous races and the spiritual countries that we will turn for guidance.

Now is a very good time to make some spiritual adjustments in our lives.

PART TWO

HOLISTIC HEALTH TECHNIQUES

Disease is as the word suggests, a dis ease of the body.

A time of imbalance.

It is not a purely physical thing but is rather an imbalance of our physical, mental, emotional and spiritual bodies.

The · mind · body · spirit · of the person.

For this reason to enjoy perfect health and peak performance the **mind, body, spirit** must be working harmoniously together.

If we were to follow a healthy food combined diet, perform gentle exercises daily and have plenty of rest, sleep and fresh air the physical body would perform well but it needs more than this to keep it up to peak performance.

Previously we have seen how thoughts and feelings are things and how, if these become negative, they can take on a denser form by blocking up the natural flow of energy in the body.

What many people do not realise is that we are composed of energy.

Our thoughts and feelings are less dense than our bodies which are dense to the point of taking on form.

However, when thoughts and feelings become dense they too take on form and actually exist in a physical sense.

This explains how physical things such as growths, tumours and infections occur in the body.

They are dense energy with physical form.

In the main we cause our own illnesses.

Even seemingly genetic illnesses can be the passing on of the mental and emotional tendencies rather than the actual physical illness.

So many of the things we say reflect this.

"A fretful child of a fretful mother."

"He's just like his father."

In many cases we take on board things which are not a part of our natural self but because we are talked into it.

How many people where cancer seemingly runs in the family are half expecting it to happen to them and are waiting for their turn?

They do.

I did it.

My mother, grandmother and several aunts died of cancer and at the age of 30 I began to lose weight drastically, have irregular bleeding and suffer from intense back pain.

My mind went to one illness - cancer - and I went through major abdominal surgery before I was convinced that this was not my problem.

It happened to be a fixed retroversion of the womb which could be rectified and was.

The question was, why did I manifest something in the same area as all my relatives?

What energy blockages did we all have related to that area, the womb, childbirth, the sexual organs?

Perhaps our blockages were not from this life time.

Perhaps we came in with them

At least I was able to break the pattern.

At the time I was in hospital almost all the women's surgical ward were there for the same reason and with the same fear.

It is a big fear among women.

We must try and **break existing belief patterns.**

We are who we are, not a likeness to someone else.

In this connection we must learn to live in the **present.**

The **past** is gone and the **future** is not yet here.

The only moment which exists is the one in which we live.

Every person would benefit from living **in the now.**

By living this moment as if it were our last and by changing old outdated belief systems and behaviour patterns is the only way we will break old patterning.

The first belief we need to change is

Disease is inevitable.

Disease is **not** inevitable.

It is self induced and only we can alter that patterning.

Change the belief to a positive one. Affirm verbally:

Good health and peak performance are available to all.

or alternatively

I only allow good health into my life.

It does not matter what the exact wording is.

It is the belief which counts and then we must set about **believing it,** not half believing it and including qualifying ifs and buts.

Our first endeavour should be to see to it that we keep our energy **flowing** in what ever way we can.

PHYSICAL METHODS

To daily practise a movement programme like the one given already or to practise recognised movement techniques which concentrate on the movement of energy such as

TAI CHI

Both of these are Chinese in origin but are finding their way into the Western world.

It is a common sight in China to see hundreds of people keeping their energy - their *Chi* flowing by simple, fluent exercises which are performed in parks, open spaces and other open areas.

Many factories and offices which employ large numbers of employees have breaks in the work time to allow people to take part in this form of exercise.

They realise that to do so is to their advantage also for the employees will work better as a result.

In the West there are many *Tai Chi* centres springing up as we begin to appreciate the value in our lives of this ancient form of exercise.

Apart from its physical benefit it also balances the mind, body, spirit for the attitude of mind and spirit when performing it is equally as important as the physical aspect.

We have a tendency in the West to dismiss something if it is not of our culture or something we discovered.

The Chinese have a very ancient culture and are very wise.

We have a lot to learn from their wisdom and it would be good for more people in the West to at least try *Tai Chi* before dismissing it out of hand.

QI GONG

This is similar to *Tai Chi* in that it too concentrates on building the person's *Chi* energy and so keeping it flowing through the body.

Qi Gong and *Tai Chi* Masters have the ability to build up massive amounts of *Chi* energy in the body and to use this to perform remarkable feats.

I was privileged to meet Dr. Effie Chow, a *Qi Gong* Master recently when we were both speaking at the same international conference in Montreal.

She performed some amazing feats of strength by using her own *Chi* energy to overcome that of others or by weakening her opponent's *Chi* energy.

One particularly impressive demonstration showed that by merely **telling** someone that they were hopeless weakens the *Chi* energy of that person.

She chose a very strong man and tested his arm strength which was far greater than her own.

She then asked the audience to say unpleasant things to him and she then tested him again.

His arm went down like a baby's.

By weakening his **self esteem** his physical strength diminished accordingly.

A sure sign that the mind affects the body.

She was able to physically move men twice her size and weight by either physically or mentally diminishing their *Chi* energy.

She has produced a very informative book which is listed in the suggested reading and which I would highly recommend.

The book also lists many **miracles** of healing she has performed by using her own *Chi* energy or helping patients to develop their own.

At one demonstration she removed my back pain by simply changing the flow of my *Chi* energy in my spine.

She did this by gently stroking away the pain.

In the West we are so accustomed to running straight to the traditional doctor when we have a pain or turning to old methods even if they are not successful, only because it is what we know and therefore we feel secure.

To change our ways means taking a leap into the unknown and this takes courage and most of the time we are locked into **fear.**

This little word keeps cropping up time and time again and yet if we were to ask someone

"Are you afraid of anything?"

They would most probably answer

"No."

The truth is we are afraid and the most obvious area is in making **changes.** My meeting with Dr. Effie Chow will always mark a significant moment in my life.

Inwardly I knew that to treat people well, to build their self esteem and to encourage rather than discourage them leads to success. It was something I had practised all my life in my teaching.

I always tried to find what the child could do and build upon this rather than criticise what he or she could not do.

However, I did this intuitively rather than by knowing what it was actually doing to the *Chi* of the person.

This has been a great discovery for me.

It also helped me to understand why my health deteriorated and I drew the back injury into my life when I did.

I was in a difficult second marriage to a recovering alcoholic who was also manic depressive. The hardest thing for me to endure was the **verbal abuse.**

Until I met Dr. Effie Chow I did not know what the effect of this can be on one's strength.

I see now why I went under . . . .

It is such a simple discovery but imagine how it can alter our lives and our understanding and tolerance of what is happening to others around us.

We tend to dismiss the difficulties of others often with casual remarks such as:

"They don't know any better."

This is a careless and uncaring remark for we all do not know everything and one simple discovery such as I made with Dr. Effie Chow might be the small thing which changes their lives.

If we consider the families with difficulties probably their biggest difficulty is their **low self esteem.**

By helping to build this we would build their *Chi* and assist in building their health.

I see the value of this small piece of knowledge as **life changing.**

I sincerely hope that all those working with families with difficulties have the chance to make this discovery and to act upon it.

REIKI

Reiki is a form of energy healing which is more similar to a "hands on" or "therapeutic touch" form of treatment.

Reiki also uses the *Chi* energy or the **universal life energy** but in a slightly different way.

In Reiki the person using the energy does not store it in his or her own body but merely acts as a **channel** for the energy to flow from the Universe to themselves or through themselves to others.

It is a form of self healing or healing of others which we are all able to do but until now have not been attuned to use properly.

Although another Eastern technique, Reiki is spreading rapidly to the West and the technique can be learnt in a few hours.

The concept is simple and the Reiki principles give positive guide lines for every day living.

These are:

Just for today I will not worry.

Just for today I will not be angry.

Just for today I will do an honest day's work.

Just for today I will show gratitude for all my blessings.

Just for today I will love and respect all living things.

To follow the *Reiki* principles alone without practising the technique would greatly improve the spiritual side of our well being and our mental and emotional approach to health.

To take the *Reiki* attunements and to always have the healing power of Reiki at your finger tips is an added advantage to the maintenance of good health.

I completed my *Reiki* Master in New Mexico several years ago and it has been a source of great pleasure to me to share this form of healing with others.

I firmly believe that if we are to take our health into our own hands and to make Total Awareness a daily part of our life we need to learn at least one self healing technique, and Reiki is simple to learn but very effective.

In Canada recently I attuned my first *Reiki* children who are now able to treat themselves with *Reiki.*

It was exciting for them and for me.

Children are very trusting and unbiased in their approach to new techniques and it had been a delight to see them practising on themselves.

What greater gift can we give our children than self healing?

I sincerely hope that more people will enquire into this technique which is relatively new to the Western world but which is spreading rapidly as more people are looking beyond the traditional methods.

Reiki has come in for some criticism in so much that because it takes so short a time to learn some people think that the prices charged for the courses are too high.

I personally do not feel that a price can be put on such a valuable gift but in my own teaching I do only teach small groups to ensure that the attunement is a personal one as I believe this to be sacred and not something to be done en masse.

Also I wait until the people "find me" for then I know that the meeting was intended and that there is a reason this person has come my way.

I have always met the people I am about to teach or have heard of them through friends.

I feel that we are already known to each other before we begin and we stay a "family" afterwards.

My *Reiki* family are very important to me.

During my time as a *Reiki* Master I have experienced many miracles in healing.

One in particular is very worthy of mention for it was the one which would dispel my doubt as to my ability to heal myself or help others to heal themselves.

Although I had no reason to doubt the power of Reiki I did doubt that I would be able to do it.

Self doubt and lack of self worth creeping in again.

I did doubt something so simple and particularly as so little training was necessary.

Whatever I have done in life has taken years of training or hours of practice and I admit to being dubious about something which did not necessitate arduous training but is effective as a result of a simple attunement.

When practising *Reiki* as a part of my Master course I had occasion to work closely with my *Reiki* Master, Gonzalo Nava.

At each session something miraculous would take place so I was obviously working in harmony with the energy but as is our way, even with all the small miracles which were occurring, I began to think that it might stop. My self doubt crept in.

At this point I developed a lump on my thyroid gland which two independent specialists diagnosed as a form of adenoma but added that they were not happy about the situation and suggested that I return to England for a biopsy.

Their worried expressions and suggestion that this could be a cancerous growth threw me into fear.

I consulted my *Reiki* Master and for 24 hours treated the area with self healing.

In addition to this:

I visualised the lump melting away.

Affirmed verbally that I did not want this thing in my body.

Prayed.

Took Rescue Remedy for the fear.

Asked the body for its co-operation.

After 24 hours I returned to the university hospital in Albuquerque, New Mexico for a scan and to everyone's amazement the lump had disappeared but where it had been was a shadow which looked like a scar.

I feel sure that this event happened to convince me that I did have the power to heal myself and to let go of any self doubt or any doubt about the healing power of *Reiki.*

This one incident has also been a valuable example to those I teach for they also go through the same feelings.

We do doubt ourselves and anything which is new to us.

We need to have more faith which is positive and leave behind our mistrust which is negative and comes from – fear.

If I look back to all the occasions in my life when I have had a medical problem I can find an underlying psychological cause of the illness.

On every occasion I have learnt something from the experience.

Maybe this is also a reason for illness.

They were all lessons disguised as illness which were essential to experience so that I may sort out the real problem.

In this way illness can be a learning aid.

In retrospect I can say thank-you to the Universe for the lessons.

It taught me something more about myself and the areas which still needed attention.

Out of interest for my readers I would like you to look back to the times that you have been ill and search around the illness for possible psychological causes which might have weakened your *Chi* energy and made you more vulnerable.

I list the causes of illnesses in my own life for these may jog your memory.

Allergies	Coincided with mine and my husband's change of job, a move to a new house, the birth of my first child and my mother's illness. **Possible cause - stress** resulting from **Fear of the unknown**
Gynaecological problems	Mother's death from cancer Father's illness and sudden death. **Possible cause - Fear** and subconscious belief that it would be my turn next.

Burns	
Abnormal cells	
in cervical smear test	**Fear of personal circumstances and being alone**
Accidents	
Injury to spine	**Unhappiness in difficult second marriage**
	***Chi* energy weakened by verbal abuse**
Eye infection	**Not wanting to see a situation. Fatigue.**

These, fortunately are the only complaints in fifty seven years but each one was not what it seemed and only in retrospect was it possible to see the real reason for the illness.

In all of the instances given if I had been aware of the cause I could have changed my reaction to the circumstances.

We can not always change the circumstances but we can change our **perception of the circumstances.**

This is why the same circumstances do not affect people in the same way.

We all perceive things differently.

In each of the given cases my perception of the circumstances was causing the illness, not the circumstances.

I only have myself to blame.

However, blame is negative and therefore we have to

forgive ourselves.

On a more positive note we can look at an example of how positive thinking can prevent disease and this again comes from my own experience.

It would seem that I could always think positive for the children in my life if not myself.

I had two children and neither one of them had a single childhood illness.

This may not seem remarkable but statistics show that it is.

When other children had measles, chicken pox, mumps, whooping cough, German measles and so on, neither child succumbed.

I can only put this down to positive thinking on my part which boosted their *Chi* energy and helped their resistance.

On a practical level I did not want them to be ill and we were in a happy, settled time in our family life so that they did have everything going for them.

What it does confirm for me is that as adults we do affect our children's lives in many unseen ways and it is our responsibility to them to get our own act together and provide them with security of mind as well as in their physical environment.

REFLEXOLOGY

Following my major back surgery I spent many weeks and months performing simple exercises to regain the mobility of my spine.

This I achieved with great success and now enjoy freedom of movement in this area.

The **pain** however was a different story and although the movement returned it was not without pain.

After the incident in hospital with the toxaemia following the use of pain killers I refused to take these and turned to **Reflexology** as a possible solution to the pain.

Reflexology is the treatment of body complaints whether they be organs or the skeletal structure through the feet.

A trained reflexologist knows all the pressure points on the feet and the area of the body with which they coincide.

It is therefore very important to go to a well qualified and reputable reflexologist, for to exert pressure on the wrong areas of the foot can cause problems rather than prevent them.

Usually the reflexologist does a foot scan by examining all the parts of the foot and making her own conclusions.

Often the reflexologist prefers not to know the problem you think you have for she may find that the situation is not what it seems.

She will make a chart of the foot marking the areas where there are energy blockages or where there are crystals and then explain which parts of the body these affect. Invariably your complaint is in there.

It takes several treatments to disperse crystals but eventually these break up and as the energy flows again there is a noticeable improvement in the affected body part.

After major surgery this was the only technique which helped to alleviate the pain.

I had the traditional hospital treatments of electric waves and ultra sound but none of these was as effective as **Reflexology.**

HOMEOPATHY

At the same time as turning to Reflexology I had tried **Homeopathy** but not with a great deal of success. I realise that this was not the homeopath's fault but my own.

I was so sure that the cause of all my back pain was the physical operation that I overlooked the mental, emotional and spiritual trauma I was experiencing in the unhappy marriage.

It was not enough to treat the physical back pain.

I should have revealed what was happening in my private life but I neglected to do so, Thus the homoeopath only had half of the picture.

Years later I realise that my back pain only recurs when I have an imbalance in the mental and emotional aspects of my life.

If I were disappointed in Homeopathy at that time I would be given the chance to see what Homeopathy can achieve.

Recently, in Montreal, I had need to consult a homeopath again and was to experience another miracle of healing.

For some reason I had "taken on board" an eye infection which started as a mild allergy to the pollen but after treatment with antibiotics, which did not suit either me or the condition, blew up into a very severe conjunctivitis. When I say severe I mean severe. There was not one visible speck of white left in the eyes and it was accompanied by great pain.

After the unsuccessful treatment at the hospital with two different antibiotics they said that there was nothing more they could do and sent me home to heal naturally, which they claimed could take anything from one to five months for the conjunctivitis was very severe.

My friends in Montreal recommended Dr. Ray Pavlov a Homeopath of great ability. He had already cured one of my friend's fibroids and has had many successes in other areas with cancer and terminal illnesses.

From the onset I was impressed with Dr Pavlov's penetrating insight into the "real person".

It was obvious from the very beginning that this was a person with a highly developed intuition who did not look at the body of his patients but into the soul.

Of all the medical practitioners I have met in my lifetime in both traditional and alternative fields I would say that Dr Pavlov demonstrated the most sensitive awareness to the mind, body, spirit concept.

It was very easy to have faith in such a person and it did not surprise me that **within 3 days** the eye condition was completely cleared.

The treatment was with homeopathic drops, tablets and cream but the real treatment was the in depth study of the reason behind the complaint and his guide to adjustments in my life to prevent a recurrence.

Dr Pavlov began his career in orthodox medicine.

He is a doctor with many degrees and a successful career in traditional medicine but he has found it possible to achieve **greater success with homeopathy than surgery** and the former is, of course, less traumatic for the body.

He is an outstanding example of his work and I regard it a great privilege to have met him.

Indeed I thank the Universe for the eye infection.

It was worth a few days of discomfort and fear to meet with such a remarkable person.

ACUPRESSURE

It is not uncommon for different holistic practices to employ acupressure as a complementary part of their treatment.

In his treatment with Homeopathy Dr Pavlov also looks at the outer ear and examines this carefully for the different organs and their condition can be diagnosed from this.

If there was a problem he would apply pressure to the point.

Dr Effie Chow in her *Qi Gong* also uses acupressure and devotes a good proportion of her book to a description of the points in the body.

By flexing your fingers at the first joint, not the knuckles, and by seeing where the middle and ring finger touch the palm an acupressure point can be found.

By rubbing the two hands together so that the two acupressure points are stimulated is a means of getting the *Chi* energy flowing.

An instant build up of heat is felt in the hands and throughout the body and when the hands are separated a few inches it is possible to experience an energy between the hands.

This is the *Chi.*

It is immediate proof that such energy exists.

Also in the webbed area, between the thumb and first finger is another pressure point which, if it is stimulated by a gentle pinching between the thumb and first finger of the other hand, will stimulate the *Chi* energy to flow.

Whenever you are feeling tired activating these two points will help to build up the *Chi* again.

At the height of my fear during the eye infection, for at first I was sure my eyes were permanently damaged, I applied pressure to these two points and could feel my energy building. I did this because I realised afterwards that one reason for the eye infection was **fatigue.**

These are only two points on the body which have a general effect on building the *Chi* but there are points all over the body which coincide with the organs and the skeletal structure and to apply pressure to these works like reflexology and reaches the affected part although that part is not actually touched.

There are many good books on acupressure but it is advisable to follow them very carefully. Acupressure is also widely used to prevent facial ageing and is a very preferable alternative to cosmetic surgery.

Not only does it give a more youthful appearance, but it works on the muscles which support the skin and is therefore more lasting. Added to which it does not involve the trauma of surgery.

Recently I was asked to give a Reiki treatment to a girl and her complaint was not know to me.

I noticed at the onset that she had received plastic surgery to her face but this was not what she had asked to be treated for.

However, in Reiki the body reveals where its real problems are and the causes of the associated problems, and my firm feeling was that the cause of all her other traumatic complaints was her face.

Although she told me otherwise at first, it transpired later that she had silicone implants in her cheeks and these began to break up, causing lumps which started to push through the skin. She had already received two complete skin grafts to her fact and was contemplating another.

She needed more corrective treatment for the cosmetic surgery than the cosmetic surgery had involved.

Perhaps if she had known about acupressure and how the skin's vitality can be restored in this way she may have avoided the cosmetic surgery in the first place.

There is no quick way to effective on going health and beauty.

It can be achieved by lovingly caring for the Mind, Body, Spirit.

ACUPUNCTURE

Acupuncture works on the same principles as acupressure only in this case needles are inserted into the pressure points.

It is a form of medicine which has been used in China for thousands of years and depends for its effectiveness on the practitioner having an exact knowledge of the meridians of the body which are the pathways through which the energy flows.

By applying needles to the blocked energy points the *Chi* energy is stimulated and encouraged to flow again.

I would not suggest that anyone try acupuncture on themselves.

Great care must be taken in the cleanliness of the needles and in an age of HIV, when there are risks from injections of any sort, it is advisable to ensure that the practitioner of Acupuncture is working under ideal conditions with clean, sterilised needles.

I have not recommended anything in this publication that I have not personally tried and found to be effective.

Between 1984 and 1986 my work involved a lot of driving as I was then the choreographer to the Welsh Ice Skating Squad and drove 5 hours a day from Northern England to Wales.

This was on top of a 7 hour coaching session.

By the time I returned at night my neck and shoulders were very stiff and painful.

Reluctantly I tried acupuncture for I was fearful of the needles but with one session I noticed a distinct improvement in the pain.

I continued with the treatments as and when I needed them.

It is interesting to note that in England, today, some traditional doctors are not only advocating acupuncture but are including it in their traditional practice.

Our local village doctor is one such person.

The gap between traditional and complementary medicine is narrowing and it is heartening that doctors are recognising that alternative techniques can complement their own.

BACH FLOWER REMEDIES

Increasingly in natural healing people are turning to natural remedies from the plant kingdom.

These may be flowers or herbs.

Of all the **flower remedies** perhaps the best known are the **Bach Flower Remedies.**

Dr Edward Bach was a Harley Street physician who discovered by chance how ailments he possessed were relieved when he was in Nature and among specific flowers.

He went on to make tinctures from the plants and experimented first upon himself with great success.

With the co-operation of some of his patients he began to introduce them to the remedies with equally good results.

What he had noticed over the years in his traditional medicine was that patients fell into specific groups according to what emotional types they were.

High on the top of his list were patients who were **fearful.**

He went on to list several emotional or mental causes of illness and provided a flower remedy for each.

We are all very different in our make up and one of the advantages of the Bach Flower Remedies is that **personal remedies** can be made to counteract several areas which need help.

Sometimes we have a very obvious imbalance.

My own is impatience and it is not surprising to learn that the flower remedy is Impatiens, for the flower remedies work like homeopathy in so much as minute doses are given and it is impossible to overdose on any one remedy.

Behind impatience is possibly fear that if we do not do something now it might not get done.

Or maybe there is mistrust that if we do not do it no one else will.

Even the simplest little quirk of personality can be another fear. There are flower remedies for all sorts of personality quirks.

It is possible to visit a flower remedy practitioner who will ask a lot of questions and you may have to fill in a questionnaire.

The only problem with this is that most people do not know themselves well enough to answer the questions honestly.

We like to acknowledge our good points but we do not always want to see the shadow side.

I was interested, two years ago, when I was in New Mexico, to come across someone who had linked the Bach Flower Remedies with astrology and in particular with the **natal chart.**

Our natal chart shows where all the planets are at our birth and as this person was to show, this gives a true account of who we are because it takes into account our shadow side which is the area from which most of our problems stem.

My own consultation was a very accurate resumé of the aspects of me which cause the problems and highlighted impatience yet again.

From an astrological Bach Flower remedy even greater accuracy can be achieved, for our personal dishonesty as to what we really are does not get in the way.

Another feature of the Bach Flower Remedies is **Rescue Remedy.**

This is a remedy Dr Bach produced for people who were in shock or showing signs of fear.

Four drops under the tongue has an immediate calming effect and brings the body back into balance.

As with all holistic healing Dr Bach's remedies treat the whole person and for this reason the remedies work on the Mind, Body, Spirit.

They are perfectly safe to use and can even be used on young babies.

They are particularly soothing for children who are afraid or nervous.

GEMSTONE REMEDIES

These work in the same way as the flower remedies in so much as they originate from a natural source, in this case, **gemstones.**

For this reason they carry the name of the gemstone, i.e. **Aquamarine** which is for emotional insecurity and like the Bach Flower Remedies their originators have matched a gemstone remedy to a specific emotional complaint and the aquamarine is just one example.

One particular product which I have used comes from the Netherlands, from the Endelsten company whose address appears in the glossary.

As with all natural products it is best to see a practitioner who is trained in these things as it can save a lot of time and expense.

HERBAL REMEDIES

Herbal medicine has been with us for generations.

In indigenous societies it is often the only form of medicine.

In Romany societies the hedgerow has provided the herbs for their healing and Gypsy Remedies are still used in England.

My first introduction to the amazing healing properties of herbs was through a friend in Spain who cured herself of cancer with herbs and introduced me to the Maria Trebin books.

Another incredible person and a pioneer in the field of Herbal therapy, Maria Trebin has case histories which fill numerous books and all refer to her personal cures.

The cures are outstanding.

Her books would be a valuable inclusion in any family library of health.

A simple introduction to herbal therapy is through drinking herb teas.

These are readily available in shops today and there are simple books on their use for each tea does have a specific use.

They are refreshing, non toxic and cleansing and can have different effects, depending upon whether they are stimulants or sedatives.

A certain amount of care should be taken in choosing them for some are laxatives and this could be unpleasant.

If they are too acidic a little honey or maple syrup can be added to make it smoother to the taste.

AROMATHERAPY

A very pleasant way to experiment with holistic healing is to satisfy the sense of smell.

By appealing to this single sense a change of mood can occur
A pleasant bath using aromatic oils or a body massage using your favourite aromatic oil can do a great deal to relax the body and mind. It is often enough just to have an oil burner in a room to give out the aroma of your choice.

Like other preparations already mentioned, the aromatic oils have specific effects on the body, depending upon the type.

Some are relaxing.

Others are stimulating.

Some are aphrodisiacs. It is personal preference and it also depends upon the effect you wish to achieve as to the choice made.

The combination of aromatherapy and relaxing, inspirational music can do a great deal to harmonise the body.

When I was in Iowa in 1996 I came across the work of Gary Young, who at the age of 24 had an accident which let him paralysed.

He refused to accept that he would be paralysed for life and studied haematology, medicine, anaesthetics, acupuncture, pathology, nutrition, herbalism and many other healing modalities. The result of his research is that he has drawn together all this experience into his work as an aroma- therapist but his work differs from others in that he has pioneered and researched his own oils and health supplements.

At the present time these products are not available in England but it is hoped to bring them to Europe in the future.

His book *"Aromatherapy - The Essential Beginning"* can be obtained from the address in the resources section.

HEALING WITH COLOUR AND SOUND

There is no doubt that what we see and hear affects our well being and as people are more aware of this they are attempting to surround themselves with colours and sounds which will enhance the way they feel.

In the body we have 7 chakras.

The chakras are spinning discs of energy situated along the spine from the head to the base of the spine.
It is through these areas that we take energy into the body.

The 7 chakras respond to 7 colours.

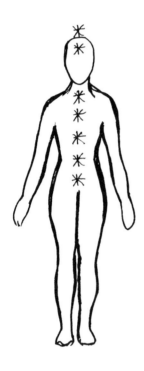

Red   Base chakra
Orange   Sacral chakra
Yellow   Solar Plexus chakra
Green   Heart Chakra
Blue   Throat Chakra
Indigo   Third Eye Chakra
Violet   Crown Chakra

Various methods can be used to stimulate these chakras by the use of colour either with crystals of these colours placed over the chakras, coloured light beamed on to the chakras, coloured materials or cards being used to stimulate the eyes to absorb more of these colours.

New and intriguing ways are being created all the time.

The colours of treatment rooms and the clothing of the practitioner can affect the mood of the client.

As individuals we often reveal more about ourselves by the colours we wear than by anything else.

We can affect and change our moods by the colours we wear.

The colour practitioner will also be able to tell you which colour type you are.

Depending upon the colours we like we fall into

Spring

Summer

Autumn

Winter

types with the corresponding personality type.

It is an amazing revelation to find out that we are a colour type and how it can affect us.

It is important to remember this when planning the decor of a home or place of work.

I did not know this when I planned the nursery of my first child. I opted for yellow as I did not know whether we would have a boy or girl.

It seemed to be a very apt choice for my first child. Stephen was very "sunny" natured, a very easy baby to rear and always happy and content.

Did the colour of his room affect him or would he have been that way anyway?

I like to think it gave him a sunny environment if nothing else.

SOUND

Just as we respond to colour we also respond to sound.

In fact as individuals **we resonate to different tones.**

We all have a tone which is harmonious with us and us with it.

Sometimes when sounds or a collection of sounds is very harsh to our ears and we feel ill at ease it is because the sounds are not compatible with our individual **sound resonance.**

Hearing too much of a sound or collection of sounds with which your body does not resonate can be **harmful to the balance of the body.**

Equally so to hear sounds that are your resonance can have soothing, balancing effects on the body.

A sound practitioner will help you to find your personal tone so that you can surround yourself with music which resonates with you.

Think how valuable this would be for fretful children.

We have placed ourselves and our children in so many situations which do harm to the balance of our bodies.

Now with a little more knowledge we can attempt to rectify these situations.

Our own tone around us is very beneficial to our well being but if this is not possible harmonious music of any tone will greatly help. On a general level you would not find something soothing if it were not already very close to your own tone.

Bernie Siegal in his book *"Love, Medicine and Miracles"* has interesting things to say about the use of music in the operating theatre.

When surgery is necessary he insists that inspirational music is played throughout the operation for it is his belief that the unconscious patient is affected on a sub conscious level by what he or she hears.

He believes that there is a healing quality to music and that even during surgery a lot of the trauma to the body can be alleviated.

He takes this one stage further and also insists that the medical team speak positively throughout the operation of the patient's ability to heal and he goes as far as to say that their comments can actually affect how much the patient bleeds.

He also insists that any comments about the patient are good ones to help build his or her self esteem, even though they are asleep.

This concept agrees with that of Dr. Effie Chow's belief and proof that to talk badly about a person lowers their self esteem and thus weakens their *Chi.*

This is something we should all consider seriously for we can do a lot of harm with words.

If there is nothing good to be said about a person perhaps we should follow the advice

"If you have nothing good to say – say nothing."

This way the world may stay a little more positive.

INSPIRATIONAL MUSIC

Of all the inspirational music I have heard in recent years the music of Robert Haig Coxon, a Canadian composer, is outstanding.

I was fortunate that the Universe put me down in the home of Robert and his family and I was able to experience first hand this fine artist composing and recording his latest album, *"The Silent Path"*.

It was a wonderful experience to watch the love and dedication which he put into his work and to enjoy the final result.

His music is used in clinics, hospitals and surgeries across Canada.

Indeed it is used in many other areas where there is stress.

The effect of his music with its intricate blend of harmonies and instruments is totally balancing and a must for anyone who is looking for self healing through sound.

BIORHYTHMS

Biorhythms are not so much a healing technique as an aid to understanding ourselves better.

They relate to our rhythm of life which can be drawn on a chart and shows three different lines which represent our **mental, emotional and physical** rhythms.

The three rhythms flow through our lives creating a pattern of waves.

Depending upon how the three rhythms interplay with each other we can experience highs and lows or more balanced times which are neither high nor low.

The danger time for us is when we move from a positive phase into a negative one.

That is when the lines cross the mid line drawn horizontally across the chart.

If they do this at the same time this is a **triple critical**

If two cross it is a **double critical**

If only one crosses, it is still a time to **take care.**

When all three rhythms are high together and in the positive zone this is a **high.**

When all are low together in the negative zone this is a **low.**

In the **highs** almost anything can be accomplished as everything is going for you on all counts.

During a **low** it is more difficult to accomplish things as the odds are against you.

This is why **rest** periods should be observed.

To work with your biorhythms but not be a slave to them is the best policy. It is advantageous to know in advance when a high is coming up and thus to plan important things for this time.

Also it is advantageous to know if a low is coming up so as not to overtax yourself at this time.

I have used Biorhythms in my life and the lives of my gymnasts for the past twenty years.

They have helped me personally, particularly when I have had to "rise to an occasion". I have found them invaluable and a positive aid to harmony with one's self.

It is possible to have compatibility charts done for partners and work colleagues or any occasion when people are working in close contact.

In Japan, Biorhythms are used to give greater productivity in industry.

They are also used to prevent accidents.

Particularly if they are involved in using dangerous machinery, employees are sent home if they are experiencing a triple critical.

This is because statistics show that accidents are more likely to happen on triple criticals.

In consequence work output is threatened so it is safer to send the person home.

This is balanced out when the worker is on a high for he or she is then expected to work overtime.

Work output increases because the individuals are capable of more work.

In the Western world biorhythms are used by some air lines to prevent accidents which are the result of pilot error.

It is not advisable for a pilot to fly if he is on a triple critical.

Statistics show that this is a time when air disasters due to pilot error happen.

Until I knew about biorhythms there seemed no logical explanation why a performer could give a flawless performance one day and be a walking disaster the next.

Her move from the positive to the negative in her biorhythms explained this and it was best not to pressurise her on the low days but to allow her to work at a less demanding level.

Biorhythms are a great asset in understanding your day to day fluctuations and to be able to adapt accordingly.

NUMEROLOGY

Numerology is the science of numbers and how they occur in our lives.

It is a very ancient science which was highly regarded and recognised in previous civilisations.

The ancient Egyptians built all their dwellings and temples based upon sacred geometry which is based on the use of numbers.

In our own lives it has an importance in so much as the letters of our name have a corresponding number and thus different names have different strengths and weaknesses.

The date of your birth has a meaning in numbers and makes up your destiny number which indicates what you can expect from this lifetime if you choose to follow your destiny.

It is a remarkable science and is uncanny in its accuracy.

Ten years ago I could not have prophesied the pattern my life would take and yet I should know more than anyone else about my own life. I had a numerology projection done for the years 1986-1996 and it has been deadly accurate showing happenings which I would never have considered likely, let alone possible.

I continue to keep a close account of the numbers which occur in my life and to record the outcomes It is fascinating.

I would recommend to anyone to have a numerology reading.

It will help you to understand yourself and your journey in this life time.

If nothing else, it helps to see that life is not a haphazard event but that it has a logical, predictable course if we know more about the numbers in our lives and their meaning.

We choose our names before we are born just as we choose our parents and the life situation into which we come.

In choosing our names and the time of our birth we choose what will be best for this journey on Earth.

It is a powerful concept but is true.

ASTROLOGY

Astrology like numerology is a very ancient science and previous civilisations used this to guide them in their lives.

As we have become more technical in our society we have turned less to the wonders of the universe, but there is evidence to show that this trend is reversing as more and more people are turning to astrology, and showing a greater interest in their connection with the Universe.

The influences of the planets at the time and date of our birth will greatly affect our journey in this lifetime.

To understand yourself or your children fully it is important to have a natal chart which shows the position of the planets at your birth and how they will affect you.

It is not enough to know under which sun sign you were born, which is what the daily papers give and which is why they can be very hit and miss in their predictions, for this is just one twelfth of the whole picture.

It is the combination of the position of all 12 planets which needs to be known, also their position in the houses and which are rising signs and so on.

Until I had my own natal chart drawn there were facets of my personality I did not understand. With the astrological information to hand it was easier to work out problem areas and at least to know what was causing the problem.

To have the birth charts of your parents helps too. We chose them for a reason.

The first time anyone informs you that you choose your birthday to fulfil your destiny and your parents to learn the lessons that have to be learnt from them, it is an awe inspiring thought, but once this truth is accepted it is a great deal easier to get on with living the life we came here to live.

Nothing is by chance in life.

We come from an ordered Universe and it is back to an ordered Universe that we will return.

The space in between which we call **life** can be ordered or haphazard.

We can achieve our goals and live out our pre-destined path or we can choose otherwise.

The choice is ours.

Maybe it was just my curious nature which led me to be interested in the "fringe sciences" and the "holistic healing" techniques.

It will not come as any surprise to learn that it was featured in my natal chart.

This apart, I hope that my interest and experience will have been food for thought for my readers and may send them on a journey of discovery into previously uncharted realms.

52 DAY CYCLES

During a recent visit to Montreal I was privileged to meet Dr Christopher Eriksson whose work is in health education and counselling.

He introduced me to the concept of the **52 day cycles** which run through our lives and have a significant part to play in the form our lives take.

These are the findings of H Spencer Lewis and are fully explained in his book *"Self Mastery and Fate with the Cycles of Life"*.

As with biorhythms, the cycles of life are calculated from the day of your birth and remain the same throughout life, giving periods which vary in their effectiveness for different things.

For instance there are good and bad times to sign contracts, travel, make permanent changes, start anything new, speculate, write or be creative, buy and sell, take holidays or plan relaxation, be successful, mix with the same or the opposite sex, give talks, meet people and so on.

There is also a particularly disruptive cycle when everything breaks down before it can be started anew.

To be aware of these cycles is to be in harmony with the natural flow of the body and your own personal destiny.

What intrigued me particularly was to look at my own cycles for the previous year and to compare the cycles with what I had actually done **intuitively** during those times, for I firmly believe that if we keep in tune with our intuition we will do the right things at the right time anyway. It came as no surprise to find that by keeping in touch with my intuition and doing what felt right at the time, I had conformed with the natural flow of my own 52 day cycles.

It was also interesting to see that all the major "breakdowns" in my life, ie. marriages, changes of career, break down in relationships and partnerships, whether business of pleasure, were all during this time.

Also when comparing the cycles with the biorhythm chart, it could be seen that the "highs" on the biorhythm chart coincided with the positive phases on the cycles and during the break down period for the cycles there were lows on the biorhythms too.

A very brief outline of the cycles is given here but a greater understanding can be achieved from reading H Spencer Lewis' book available from the Rosicrucian library

Cycle 1   Advance personal interests especially with people in authority

Cycle 2   Good for short duration journeys with immediate importance.
Good for change of home or business premises, but not on a permanent basis.
Not good for speculation or borrowing.

Cycle 3   High physical energy.
Not a good time to deal with women.
Good communication time.
Avoid arguments and confrontations.

Cycle 4   Psychic side prevalent.
Write or be creative.
Act upon impulse.
Be careful not to be deceived.
Not a good time to marry.

Cycle 5   Personal affairs expand, grow and increase in prosperity.
Good for long journeys.
Good metaphysical and philosophical time.
Good time to deal with lawyers.
Avoid dubious deals.

Cycle 6   Holiday period.
           Pleasure, amusement and relaxation.
           Good period to deal with women.
           Good for speculation.

Cycle 7   Disruptive period.
           Break down to rebuild.
           Not good for starting anything new.
           Avoid being impulsive.

The cycles are calculated from the person's birth date being day one of the first cycle.

WOMEN'S WELL BEING

I was in the process of trying to find a **natural** source of **progesterone** for myself as I had passed through the menopause without any problems but at the age of 56 had two recalls for smear tests and mammograms with what were described as unusual cells or changes in cellular structure.

A simple explanation for this is ageing.

However, as I have never taken chemicals into my body by choice, I did not want to go on to HRT - Hormone Replacement Therapy - as nothing convinces me that artificial hormones are good for my body.

Eventually I came up with a source of **natural progesterone** taken from the **yam** plant and available without a prescription in Eire.

The name of the company which distributes this and other health products is the Natural Health Ministry and their address appears in the resources section.

They have products for men also but in the main they deal with female well-being products.

Also, I have had cause to turn to the healing properties of **Aloe Vera** in recent months.

In the Resources section is the address of the West of England Aloe Centre but also there is now a video available by Dr. Ivan Danhof called "Remarkable Aloe". It costs £8.50 including post and packing and the video reveals Aloe Vera's properties and what constitutes good and constantly effective Aloe. Dr. Danhof also discusses major applications for its use, internally in the body, including arthritis, high blood pressure, cholesterol, bone healing, gastro- intestinal problems, liver and kidney function and the immune system.

He describes how it works beneficially on all skin types and many skin problems, details some case histories and reflects on the future of this humble but incredibly potent plant.

PART THREE

PEAK PERFORMANCE
FOR THE ATHLETE AND PERFORMER

TALENT

If you are an athlete or a performer and you are reading this you must already have talent, determination and the ability to work hard.

Your present success is influenced greatly by the amount that each of these features in your individual make up.

It is essential to possess all of these and preferably that they occur in equal proportions.

THE NATURAL

In every sport or expressive art form there will appear from time to time a Natural.

These blessed individuals come into this life with all the attributes necessary to succeed in their chosen athletic path.

It is said, and I believe it, that the **true natural,** the one who borders on being a genius in their chosen realm, is often a **reincarnated soul who has followed the same path in previous lifetimes.** A Natural does not only come in this time with the talent but also with the physique required.

The latter is vital to success and to begin one's chosen path with the correct physique is indeed a gift from above.

The concept of Naturals being reincarnated souls may surprise you but I have experiences from my own lifetime which convince me of this.

In this lifetime I was a Natural for classical ballet.

A classical dancer requires a very specific physique comprising:

>   Naturally slim body
>   Long legs
>   Delicate bone structure
>   Small hands and feet
>   Small head
>   Long neck
>   Expressive eyes
>   High cheek bones
>   Slender muscles.

She also needs:
>   Musicality and a sense of rhythm

Combined with:
>   Dramatic ability

And finally, **SOUL.**

This is quite a demanding list.

On top of this she requires:
>   The ability to work alone
>   Self Discipline
>   Attention to detail
>   Intelligence.

On top of all this she must enjoy physically demanding, hard work.

It was my make up to possess these qualities and not surprisingly I took to ballet like "a duck to water".

I did not need any parental pressure.

This was my choice and my joy of expression.

My first feelings that I had done all this before came early when I always seemed to know in advance what was required and had a natural feel for new exercises.

Ballet is not executed from the mind, it has to be **felt.**

This "knowing" of having danced before was more evident when I performed in a theatre for the first time for I knew all the names for the parts of the stage although I had not been on stage before.
The wings, the prompt corner, the backdrops were all familiar words as was the music.

My parents were not classical music enthusiasts but I recognised and could name classical pieces.

Later in my career when I was still only twelve, I would begin singing lessons and embarrass the teacher and composer with whom I worked by being able to sing things the adults could not sing.

This may seem like a gift but it leads to a lot of friction with other artists.

Indeed all my early ballet years seemed like a "re-run" but I feel that in this lifetime my journey was not to be a performer but a teacher.

In more recent years when discussing Naturals I have occasion to think of a gymnast who came to my club after I had retired from competitive work and so I did not work with her.

I have reason to believe that she was the reincarnation of one of the Bulgarian gymnasts killed in the air crash which wiped out the whole team and their coach.

She came into the club I had formed and took to Rhythmic Gymnastics like a duck to water.

Most surprisingly she had a Bulgarian style.

As this was after I had left the club I did not have the pleasure of coaching her but feel that my role was to provide the club in the first place so that she would have a place into which to come and also to provide her with at least 25 colleagues who had all trained in Bulgaria. This was unusual for we were the only club, apart from one other, who had trained with the World Champions in Bulgaria.

You can call it coincidence but it is a big coincidence.

These are only two of my own experiences but I have heard of many others.

They are relevant to the text for apart from showing that these things do happen it helps the Natural to understand some things he or she might not otherwise understand.

I had a lot of difficult years as a child because of this talent.

Among your colleagues it does not make for friendships and creates a lot of jealousy.

It is not an easy feeling knowing that those around you are waiting for you to make a mistake just to show that you are not as wonderful as everyone thinks.

Naturals do occur but it is a challenging situation for coach and performer alike.

A Natural does not need a lot of coaching.

In fact a Natural probably knows more than the coach. This can be a demanding realisation for the Ego.

The Natural does not need as much practice as the technique is already there.

They can often appear lazy, causing friction between the coach and performer.
The apparent lack of effort and need to train can cause problems with other performers.

It seems to them that the Natural gets to shine without the same amount of work.

This is a truth.

The Natural will shine with less work because the Natural has everything on her side.

However, she will also have to learn that being a Natural has its disadvantages as it can cause jealousy and resentment with which the Natural has to learn to live.

Thus to be a Natural is not as enjoyable as it might at first seem.

It is a sensitive training relationship and one which should be recognised early and treated with sensitivity.

The Natural should not be singled out at group training but she does need one to one tuition.

Private lessons and sessions are a must if the best pupil/coach relationship is to be achieved, and others should know the reason for this.

In my coaching experience I did not encounter a Natural, but having been one I count this a blessing rather than a disappointment.

The Natural's road is a lone one and I was happy to have children with other characteristics which made for a happy working relationship and which could be developed more harmoniously.

I mention the Natural only because you may be one or you may have to coach one or you may have to work alongside one.

Being a Natural does not give anyone an easy ride.

A Natural has to be made of stern stuff on the inside to take the knocks and often their supreme sensitivity means that they are not tough enough to do this.

I would ask all those who have a Natural in their midst to treat them with great sensitivity.

Their outward ability is not always felt inside and they can spend vast amounts of time feeling insecure and fearful as they do not have the maturity to handle the talent.

THE WORKER

At the other end of the scale to the Natural is the Worker.

The performer or athlete who gets there through effort.

Often these people have not got the perfect physique and may have to work hard and long to correct body faults but they have the qualities necessary to succeed, i.e. determination and the ability to work hard.

Determination and the ability to work hard

In my years of coaching I came to the conclusion that

25% talent plus 75% effort

took performers to the top equally as well as
75% talent and 25% effort.

To go to the top in any physical art form or sport is gruelling.

There is no letting up on mind or body and if you are a performer of the 25% talent and 75% effort category do not feel overshadowed by those who seemingly have more talent.

They can not succeed without effort.

I would ask performers of the Worker category to always value your self worth.

You may not have the natural attributes but you have an unbeatable strength in your courage and determination to succeed, which will not only assist you in your chosen sport but also in your life.

I would ask coaches and teachers to value these performers greatly.

They are the back bone of any club or school.

THE IDEAL

Ideally for all concerned the ideal performer is one with

50% talent and 50% effort

but these are few and far between.

50% talent and a potentially good physique can be developed with good training to become nearly perfect.

We can not alter bone structure but we can alter almost everything else.

Combined with consistent effort it is possible to create a performer with great potential.

I would ask my readers to consider where they or their pupils fit into these categories, for to know who you are in sport is the same as in life.

We have to know where we fit in and how to work with our limitations or assets, whichever apply.

In my work my time was spend in the early years with

Recreational performers followed in later years with

Competitive performers.

The work is very different and demands a totally different approach on both sides.

THE RECREATIONAL PERFORMER

My recreational work was in my school of physical arts which included dance, drama, gymnastics and yoga but the emphasis was placed upon the joy of performance without the pressure of exams or competitions.

This did not mean that the standard was not high, for each child realised his or her own full potential, but there was more time devoted to expression rather than to technique.

Of all my teaching experience I regard these as very valuable, creative and spiritual years.

I know that I grew from the experience and feel sure that the children and their families did too.

In the search for physical excellence we often lose sight of the joy and when something becomes mechanical and from the mind rather than the soul a great deal is lost.

To be able to keep a balance of Mind, Body, Spirit in training is equally as important as in health.

For this is training the whole person.

It is therefore "Wholistic".

The recreational performer should not be considered by herself or coach inferior to the competitor. The recreational performer is performing at a level best sited to his or her needs and the added bonus of this is that it is always a joy.

Even hard work is a joy if there is no pressure attached.

Like the Worker, the Recreational performer is the back bone of any club or school.

THE COMPETITOR OR PERFORMING ARTIST

After my school of physical arts I went on to form a school of excellence for Rhythmic Gymnastics which, although it had a recreational section at the beginning, resulted eventually in being a school of excellence for 25 gymnasts.

When we had a recreational section a certain degree of balance was maintained and there were times when training was less pressurised and it was enjoyable all the time.

Eventually with a school of excellence for 25 girls the tables had to turn as all attention was on competitions and grade exams.

When all the attention is on success it is hard to maintain a balance between Joy of performance and Excellence of performance.

If top performers and coaches are honest the joy does go out of the window when all attention is focused on greater skill and artistry.

The competitor and artist must be prepared to work very hard, often without the freedom to let go for even a second.

It depends how dedicated and committed coach and performer are, but it is a long, hard road to the top with little chance of experiencing moving for the sheer joy of moving.

It is a choice that has to be made only after careful consideration.

The only way a balance can be achieved is to devote some time, classes and training to expression rather than technical excellence.

One of my own reasons for retiring from competitive gymnastics in 1985 was because it was no longer a joy to me.

The children were always a joy and the teaching likewise, but the back biting and dissatisfaction at national and international level took away the pleasure.

It was with reluctance on my part for the children that I retired and I miss the joy they brought into my life and the happy shared experiences we had, but this did not counteract the bitterness of competition and performance at peak level.

This is something I mention at this point to illuminate the areas about being a peak performer that are not as glossy as may at first appear.

It is very ego building to be the best at what you do but in being the best other sacrifices have to be made.

Realising one's goals and ambitions is creditable but it is good, once in a while, to stand back from the situation and take stock of how this is affecting the balance of your life.

Are you still able to be whole?

Are you balanced in Mind, Body and Spirit?

Is the physical search for excellence stunting your spiritual growth?

I am not passing judgement on the competitive world, merely asking those embarking on it or involved in it to take stock from time to time.

Another aspect of peak performance which can not be overlooked is the sacrifices that have to be made at a family level.

All training, when done to an extreme, costs money - and it gets more costly.

It usually involves travel which is both costly and time consuming. It involves special clothing and equipment which is again costly and last but not least it is very demanding on the family's time.

It is vital to have **family support** in the early days and to have **partner support** in the later years.

I have seen superb performers give up because these conditions could not be met.

This applies to coaches and teachers too

It can be a very lonely road if one endeavours to make it alone

It is something to consider very seriously at the onset for the peak performer often has to sacrifice everything to make it to the top.

MIND POWER IN TRAINING

We are assuming now that after reading the less glossy aspects of peak performance you still want to proceed.

This shows you have determination, are not easily shaken and have mind power.

The latter is something which has to be developed if you are to maintain peak performance.

The mind is a very powerful tool and when kept positive can achieve the impossible.

The impossible is only impossible because others say it is.

To the positive mind anything is possible.

In training it is very important:

    a. to set goals

    b. to keep a training book

    c. to set a training routine which can be practised at 100% effort.

Setting goals

Your goal will not be the same as your training partner.

No two people are alike.

You may be going in the same direction but not necessarily in the same way.

Set goals on:

    1. Achieving physical excellence through body conditioning

    2. Achieving technical excellence

    3. Achieving joy and expression in performance.

All of these can be done by **writing down** the goals.

Put them into concrete form by repeating them **verbally.**

Doing this enables the brain to recognise that you mean business.

When once you have physically and mentally accepted your goals then set out to use your mind power to achieve them.

Some basic guides to this are:

Whenever a negative thought about your goals comes into your head dismiss it with three positive ones about yourself.

This often happens when you get a hang up that something is not good or that you can't do it.

Think of three things you can do well and start thinking positive again.

Always when training keep your self esteem high.

Even if your coach is being hard on you

keep your self esteem high.

Low self esteem weakens your *Chi* and thus your strength.

Self belief strengthens your *Chi.* Know that by continually programming the mind to achievement you will achieve.

The body wants to please you. It is pleased you have respect and admiration for it.

Allow it to express this.

Do not place upon it limitations that are the suggestion of others.

Listen to your coach but most of all

Listen to your body.

Always focus on **the best you can do.**

Do not compare yourself with others except to raise your own goals.

If you admire someone because they have more skill do not leave it as admiration - make that level of excellence **your goal.**

The mere fact that someone has a level higher than your own shows that it is possible.
Never feel **defeated** or **inferior.**

Everything is a passing state and can change.

I distinctly remember moving up from children's ballet grades to major examination work. I was 13 at the time and very thin,

I had legs like a foal which were long and spindly.

I moved into a class of mature girls who were well developed and strong.

I felt like a puny amateur in their midst.

I gazed awe-struck at the height of their arabesques, and the strength of their beats and turns and temporarily I felt deflated. It did not help that they were amused by the skinny little individual who had dared to begin major work.

A little voice inside of me perked up with 3 positive things:

1. You have a natural physique
2. You have natural "line"
3. You have musicality and expression.

I took a deep breath and joined the rest of them.

Within a few months I was holding my own with them all and continued to dance long after they had given up, mainly because of their weight problems.

Without the inner voice and the training to look for 3 positive assets and believe them I might have given up on that first difficult day.

At some point in your training there will be someone better than you but use this as an incentive to bring out the best in you.

We govern our own success, no one else.

Only we know our true potential and it is up to us to nurture the **self belief and mind power** to realise this potential.

Goals will change so keep updating them.

Always in your mind be prepared in advance of what the body needs

See your body and the skill you need **in advance** of what you are now and **visualise** the perfect you performing with all the skills in advance of what you require.

The mind will start to programme this for you.

The cells of the body respond to the challenge and you will achieve it.

There is no such word as impossible

Some personal examples:

In 1980 I was teaching Artistic Gymnastics which is beam, bars, vault and floor and I had 300 pupils. I injured my right arm supporting someone on asymmetric bars and could no longer lift anyone. This could have meant the end of my club and my livelihood. I had to think quickly and I decided to switch sports to Rhythmic Gymnastics. My only connection with this had been as a visiting dance teacher / choreographer to the top club in the country at that time, which was the Leeds Athletic Institute. I had loved the sport on sight but did not have any knowledge of it apart from what I had seen at the L.A.I.

Until I could regroup my gym I had helpers to continue with the artistic section but I did a hasty switch, absorbed myself in the sport and worked on the strengths I had, which were dance training and choreography.

I set my goal.

Within 5 years we would be the British champions.

A high goal. Indeed an impossible goal some said, but **nothing is impossible if you believe in it.**

Within 5years by the summer of 1985 we were:

Under 10 years: British team champions

Under 14 years: British Team - silver medallists

Under 10 years: Individual British Champion

Winners in every National Grade

Out of an infant British Squad of 25 girls 12 of them were ours.

One gymnast performed at the European Team Event and as an individual representative at the Senior World Youth Games.

5 years prior to this all the gymnasts were raw beginners and all I knew about the sport was what I had seen.

Impossible, everyone said - but was it?

I had the **belief** that we could do it and this belief was strengthened by our combined **effort** and **love.**

On both sides there was 100% effort at all times combined with love.

My aim was to do the best I could to help my gymnasts **realise their true potential.**

It was **their personal best** which was important but this turned out to be the best in the country.

Another **miracle,** I would say, but then miracles happen daily if you really believe it.

Another example of mind power is a very personal one but I know that the gymnast concerned will agree to it being shared if it will inspire others.

One of the senior British team was in training for the British Championships and only days before the finals her young mother died suddenly while the gymnast was at a training session. This could have been a devastating situation for the gymnast. Obviously she had the support of her coach and colleagues but it did not seem likely that she would rally round enough for the event.

I remembered the cutting I had taken from a gymnastics magazine some years earlier which told of the little Bulgarian gymnast who, although her mother and all her colleagues had been killed in an air disaster, decided to "go out and perform in their honour".

She did this and was successful regardless of her overwhelming grief. Whether this cutting helped our British gymnast or whether, like the little Bulgarian, she had the guts to go out and perform against great odds, I do not know, but Jackie did go out and perform for her mother and in consequence regained her British title.

Both these occurrences are, I would say, examples of mind **power.**

THE TRAINING BOOK

Keep a daily training book which includes:

1. Your day's training. a.   What is performed
                          b. An assessment of your performance
                          c. Areas requiring attention

2. Your health   a. Any problems, physical, mental, emotional
                          b. From where do they come?
                          c. How to eliminate them

3. Diet   The day's eating pattern. Any junk food?

4. Rest and Sleep   In what proportions?

5. Relaxation   Letting-go, time to relax the body, mind and spirit.

A truthful, accurate training book keeps the performer closely in touch with himself or herself.

It is a form of self examination and a way of "nipping in the bud" things which can easily become bad habits.

The training book is also the means by which the coach can monitor what is happening in other aspects of the performer's life.

A valuable inclusion in the training book is the

Biorhythm chart

As explained earlier in the book biorhythms are the mental, emotional and physical rhythms of the person.

They are an accurate guide to how the body is behaving naturally.

Biorhythms if used positively can be a great asset to a performer.

The most important way to work with them is:

1. To maximise on the Highs
2. To be aware of the Lows.
3. To take note of Critical Days

By maximising on the highs when all aspects of your being are high it is possible to work harder and go for moves which have eluded you or until now have been out of reach.

This is always a successful time and if it is possible to arrange your own performances do them on these dates.

Competitions are usually set nationally but if a high coincides with a big competition it is a psychological boost.
Be aware of the low times when everything is negative.

Do not give up on life or training but be easier on yourself.

It is not sensible if your chart says rest, to throw yourself into something new or demanding.
The odds are not with you.

Added to which to over-train during a rest period will add to the risk of injury.

Critical Days should be observed carefully because things can change very quickly as the biorhythms cross over the line between positive and negative.

They could cross over in the middle of a training session or performance.

Be aware of this time and be more sensitive to what your body is telling you.

It is debatable whether the biorhythms are kept by the performer or by the coach.

In my case, because I was working with young gymnasts, I kept them.

In fact they and their parents did not know I used biorhythms in training but I found them invaluable as an extra aid to my own intuition.

Also if there was a big competition coming up and if there were two performers who were equal on every account except their biorhythms, it would obviously be sensible to choose the one who was on a high rather than one who was on a triple critical.

It was not often that I used them for competition as selection was made on performance often weeks ahead, but there is a value here.

The greatest value is in understanding the performer more fully.

In my life today I do still use my biorhythms. I try to work through the lows but do not over-tax myself but I do take note of the rests. Alternatively I try and maximise on the highs.

They are as useful to the non athlete as to the athlete.

ROUTINE TRAINING TO 100% EFFORT

It may be surprising to you to see that I recommend training to 100% effort for some would advocate that this be kept for performance or competition.

For my own part I found, with my gymnasts, that by expecting 100% from them in training they gave me it and it helped them to prepare themselves **in advance of their immediate needs.**

As a result they were always prepared mentally for an event when it came along as they practised to this level at every training session.

Their bodies were always in peak condition and we did not have accidents and injuries.

In all my years of coaching I did not have an injured gymnast.

This might suggest that they were not extending themselves or working to their true potential but it was the exact opposite.

They were bodily prepared beyond their immediate needs and mentally visualising potential beyond their own.

In gymnastics moves are graded according to difficulty as medium difficulties or superior moves. Although the gymnasts were aware that their exercises needed certain moves they worked at all levels of difficulty simultaneously so that they never had the mental block that something was superior.

On one occasion my youngest competitor had 14 superior moves in her exercise.

Mentally they were the same to her and she achieved them because her brain said, "they are all equal, you can do them all".

Our mind is the biggest block to our potential.

Children are not blocked in this way unless we put the blocks there. It is important to **free the mind from its limitations.**

When this is done even the less perfect body will respond.

If this is combined with a build up of **self esteem** and a healthy **respect** and **love** of the body's capabilities the potential is enormous.

It is not egotistical to keep telling the body you love it.

The body responds to love.

This does not mean physically pampering it but like a child it needs to be shown:

Respect, love, admiration and to be free to express and develop to its full potential.

Thus to train at 100% effort is possible and what it means is that when competition or performance come around the performer can relax, knowing that 100% performance is a daily routine. By relaxing they will enjoy and the enjoyment is the "missing link" which completes the picture.

The joy expresses the spiritual being and the whole picture is complete.

The result is a balanced Mind, Body, Spirit performance.

I feel quite sure that the missing link for most people has been the spiritual in competition and performance because at this level anxiety and stress creep in, mainly through trying to rise to the occasion when in fact the occasion can be in daily training.

The performance is the expression of all that has been trained.

I have lived and worked with many top coaches who are the best in what they do and have all the technical knowledge, the dedication and the years of experience but my feelings are that on a feeling level they are so bent upon success that they do not transmit the love and feeling to the performer and in constantly pressurising the performer do not create a loving relationship between them.

It is still possible to love and direct and so many potentially good working relationships are destroyed because the performer does not feel a heart connection with his or her coach.

I speak from experience as one who was "driven" towards excellence rather than nurtured towards it.

As with our children **firm guidance with love** will succeed where **ruling with a rod of iron** will fail.

Our peak performance athletes are precious people.

It is our duty to respect this and to develop them with care and consideration.

MIND POWER IN PERFORMANCE AND COMPETITION

If you have been training at 100% effort then Mind Power is a part of your every day routine.
Before a big event it is important to boost this.

On the night before at bed time **visualise success** on the following day.

If possible have a relaxed night and take time **alone** to centre yourself on the task at hand. Often at a World or Olympic Games this is not possible, but if possible do it.

On the day of the event keep to yourself as much as possible so as not to be distracted from your goal and if it is a team event stay with your team so that you have positive support.

The effect of team and spectator support is tremendous.

Whenever my gymnasts were performing I would organise one, two or three bus loads of supporters to give mental support to the gymnasts as well as verbal.

The effect of 180 people concentrating on your success is powerful.

I did not encourage them to think negative of the opposition because action follows thought and it draws in negativity in general which could have affected our own gymnasts.

Group participation is strong as long as it is positive and to the highest good.

A few minutes before you are to compete or perform mentally go through all the positive qualities you possess, highlighting all your strengths knowing that this will overshadow your weaknesses.

Breathe deeply and puff out any tension.

Let the mind and body relax into love for what you are doing.
Take more deep breaths and love yourself, your coach, your supporters and your chosen path then go out and express that love in the performance of your life.

BODY CONDITIONING

In my own training I see now that not enough time was spent on **body conditioning.**

My ballet mistress was hot on technique but to my knowledge did not have any other training outside of ballet.

I was surprised when I went as an independent choreographer to other sports how little knowledge they had of anatomy and physiology.

In retrospect I can see that my own ability could have been greatly enhanced if I had known more about body conditioning.

Maybe this influenced me in the preparation of my gymnasts for after technique my greatest emphasis was on body preparation and conditioning.

My quirk was always **to prepare the body beyond the needs of the work in hand.**

Every sport and every dance form places different requirements upon the body.

Those of you involved at these levels know what your particular sport demands.

You know which parts need to be supple and which need to be strong and you already have warm-ups and technical exercises to develop these aspects.

My own observation over the years with squads other than my own and in sports not my own is that the warm ups or Body Conditioning as I prefer to call it are too brief and do not

prepare the body beyond its immediate needs.

They do what they attempt to do, which is to warm up the body and increase blood flow so that the technical moves can be attempted but they do not advance the body in a general way which gives the performer or athlete a better vehicle with which to perform.

To give a general comparison, by systematic body conditioning of the whole body it is possible to tune up a body which is currently running like a family saloon and make it perform like a Ferrari, but this takes up valuable training time and is often discarded as time consuming.

My gymnasts were always raring to go into their skills but every training was preceded by a full hour of body conditioning.

At first they showed dissatisfaction at having to repeat the same exercises daily but little by little as they became recognised for their supreme body condition they ceased to object.

They and their parents realised that they had a tool with which to work that others had not got and this quickly took them to the fore in their sport.

In 1985 I was privileged to receive a grant from the Sports Aid Foundation in England to study with the World Champions in Bulgaria and instead of going alone I took 25 gymnasts with me.

It was an experience of a lifetime for all of us but my greatest joy was in finding that everything I had intuitively felt was necessary for the sport was in fact how the world champions were already training.

Had my gymnasts not had the attention paid to body conditioning they would have been totally out of their depth but because they were conditioned **beyond their needs** they were able to easily learn new moves.

What was also very apparent was the love which the Bulgarians shared with us as they spared top gymnasts to work with my own.

We do not need verification that what we are going is right if we are working from the intuition and from the heart.

If the intent is pure and is given with love we are approaching our work in a holistic way and the balance between mind, body, spirit is achieved, but what was reassuring in Bulgaria was to know that this was a big part of the Bulgarian training regime.

Effective body conditioning

This requires that you prepare the whole body with flexibility exercises before beginning the normal day's training.

Include all body parts even if they not feature highly in your sport.

They still need to be flexible to assist the parts that you do need. Also, a flexible body is less likely to be injured as it can react quickly to an unusual movement.

As we are dealing now with peak performers it is envisaged that you already have a body which is in good shape.

The body preparation exercises given here take the body to its maximum potential and should be attempted in moderation at first.

Where the eventual angle is 90° or 180° begin with 45° and gradually build up.

The exercises have a gymnastic bias but are equally valuable for dancers or athletes.

EXERCISE 1

PLANTAR AND DORSIE FLEXION

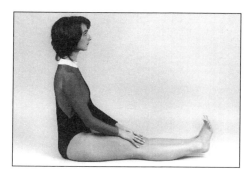

A

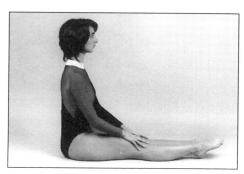

B

In long sitting with 90 degree angle in the hips point the toes down to the floor and alternately turn them up to face the ceiling.

Do this first with the heels touching the floor and then with the heels off the floor.

The latter makes the thighs work harder.

EXERCISE 2

ELBOWS TO KNEES

A

B

C

In long sitting legs straight in front.

Bend forwards to touch elbows on knees

Elbows to the sides of the knees.

Wrists to toes.

Clasp the hands and put them over the upturned feet

EXERCISE 3

HURDLE SIT FOLDS

Folds over the straight leg.

Change legs

EXERCISE 4

ADAPTED HALF LOTUS FOLDS

In adapted half lotus, one leg bent and the other straight.

Fold over the straight leg.

Change legs.

EXERCISE 5

ASSISTED LEG STRETCHES

In back lying, one leg straight and the other leg bent

Hold on to the stretched working leg and pull it over the head.

Repeat with the other leg.

EXERCISE 6

KICKS

A

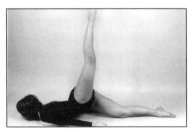

B

C

In back lying with both legs straight kicks to 45° 90° and 180° depending upon suppleness

Include front, side and back kicks

EXERCISE 7

COBRA

A

B

C

Roll on to tummy and practise the Cobra with three hand positions:

Next to the head
Next to the chest
Next to the waist

EXERCISE 8

BRIDGE

Roll on to the back, hands flat on the floor near to the ears, and feet together

Push up to bridge position.

EXERCISE 9

YOGA TWIST ADVANCED

A

B

In the Yoga twist position.

Sitting upright, one leg bent in front, heel close in to the body and the other leg bent over it, with foot flat on the ground.

Bend forwards to put head on front foot of the bent leg.

Twist away from the front leg.

Change legs.

EXERCISE 10

KICKS

A

B

C

In standing, front, side and back kicks with preparation.

Prepare by taking three steps into the kick, i.e.

right, left, right   kick

EXERCISE 11

FINGERS

KNUCKLES

FLATS

A

B

With feet together touch the fingers, knuckles and flats of hands

In front of the feet

At the sides of the feet.

Begin with feet apart if this is difficult.

EXERCISE 12

SIDE FOLDS

In straddle sit.

Side folds with the arm over the head

To Right and Left.

EXERCISE 13

FORWARD FOLDS

A

B

C

In straddle sit

Forward fold to touch the floor with

Elbows

Fore arms

Chest (eventually)

EXERCISE 14

SPLITS

Splits on right and left leg

Do not attempt if there is obvious stiffness

Wait until more suppleness is achieved through earlier forward fold exercises.

EXERCISE 15

SHOULDER SUPPLING

A

B

Arm swinging in standing

Swing forwards and backwards and back circle

Swing backwards and forwards and forward circle.

EXERCISE 16

SHOULDER SUPPLING WITH FOLD

In standing feet together.

Fingers locked behind the back.

Bend forwards and bring the arms over the head.

Attempt to get a 90° angle over the head.

Work towards 180°.

EXERCISE 17

SHOULDERS SUPPLING IN LYING

In long sitting extend the arms behind on the floor a shoulder width apart.

Aim to get as close to the floor as possible as the arms extend backwards.

EXERCISE 18

LUNGES

A

B

C

In a lunge position with the right leg forward facing to the left

Lunge to a 90° thigh level

Lunge to this level but twist the body to face the front

Lunge to put head on the floor on each bounce

Repeat with the other leg forward

EXERCISE 19

ABDOMINALS

A

C

B

From back lying with arms straight over the head and knees bent

shoot the legs straight forwards and come up to sitting bringing the arms forwards to touch the toes.

Fold forwards.

EXERCISE 20

ABDOMINALS USING ELBOWS TO KNEES

A

B

From back lying sit up to touch alternate elbows to knees.

EXERCISE 21

ABDOMINAL LEG CROSSES IN THE AIR

A   **B**

Lying on the back scissor the legs at a 90° angle to the hips.

Reduce this to a 45° angle.

The lower angles are more difficult.

Support the back by putting the hands under the seat if necessary

EXERCISE 22

COOL DOWN

Roll on to the shoulders and bring the knees to the head.

Rest in this position.

22 is a power number and these 22 exercises will help you to supple, strengthen and tone up the body prior to the exercises required for the specific sport.

Always finish with

Shaking of the hands and feet

Flexing of the fingers and toes

General shaking of the body

Head rolls to loosen the neck and shoulders

It is good to have music for this part of the body preparation and to have a set routine does mean that nothing is missed and it soon becomes as automatic as brushing the teeth.

What is more it can be fun and begins the training session in a more light hearted way which helps the performer to leave the outside world behind and to ease into the demands which are to follow.

HOLISTIC HELP

If the athlete or performer is following the guidelines given here he/she will already be working more holistically but a closer look at Section 2 will bring to mind the holistic help that is available from the areas already discussed.

There is one area of sport which has always concerned me and that is **accidents** and the practice of continuing to train on an injured body.

I do not feel that it was good luck that in over 30 years I did not have an accident or injury to any of my pupils. It was "good management" rather than "good luck".

Their attention to **body conditioning** ensured this but what troubled me was seeing others work with ankles and knees strapped up and to watch dancers dancing with injured toes, ankles, joints and backs.

It is not sensible to work with injuries.

If you are unfortunate enough to have an injury the best treatment is rest using **remedial exercises** which give gentle exercise to the injured part **while it is supported** by either a chair, table, bed or the floor.

Most of the body preparation exercises given here are performed with the **floor as a support** to the muscles.

This gives less resulting strain to the muscles.

Should the injury persist then **gentle massage** and **Homeopathic** remedies will help.

Consult a Homeopathic practitioner before rushing for the **freezing spray** or resorting to anti-inflammatory injections.

Pain and swelling are Nature's way of telling you that the body needs rest, recuperation and love.

Do not mask the symptoms with sprays and injections. Feel the pain and allow it to guide you as to the nature and depth of the injury.

Of the Homeopathic remedies **Arnica** is an excellent standby for strains, swelling and bruising.

Together with cold compresses and rest this works very quickly.

My son who is a Sports Climber recently injured his elbow and was devastated when the doctor said that the injury might put him out of climbing for weeks, if not for good.

We treated the elbow with Arnica cream and he took Arnica tables and rested the arm for two or three days and after this short time was able to go back to light training.

Seeking Homeopathic help will help to uncover the psychological reasons for the accident or injury.

At this time my son was not happy in his job and he and his girlfriend had just broken up. It could well have been that these two other aspects created a temporary imbalance in his life which manifested as imbalance in his climbing and the subsequent injury.

Maintain balance at all times in Mind, Body, Spirit.

Another simple remedy is **Silica.**

This is a mineral supplement for tissue health in the form of bones, skin, hair and nails.

Silica gives structure to all living things and is essential to the human body.

It gives support to all connective issue and it is this which often gets damaged in training.

It also protects tendons, ligaments, and the capsule around joints.

It works with calcium in bone formation and is invaluable if an injury has occurred for it will repair bones and connective tissue.

Its greatest value is as a preventative to accidents by strengthening the body.

Primrose Oil

This natural product together with **Royal Jelly** provides nourishment and lubrication to the joints and improves the condition of the skin and connective tissue.

Both these can be taken internally but come in creams also for external use.

Other valuable supplements for the joints are cod liver oil and halibut oil.

None of these products is chemical and thus harmful to the body.

DIET

Obviously the diet of the performer will be specific to the sport as the needs of each sport differ.

The weight lifter and body builder obviously need a different diet from the dancer as they are concerned with building power, but nevertheless all will benefit from food combining.

FOOD COMBINING

This has been discussed in an earlier section but it would be advisable for all performers to appraise their eating habits and to try and adapt them to include food combining.

One important thing to remember being

to leave the protein meal to the final one of the day

In this way the protein will be fully digested and able to perform its **body building** role.

A book on food combining is a must for the training bag.

Some supermarket check-outs sell little books on this.

Thus to draw all sections together my final advice to the performer is to

> **Listen to the body**
> **Look to holistic help**
> **Love what you are doing**
> **Believe in yourself**
> **Enjoy your competitive life for it is short**

It has been my endeavour throughout this book to keep it simple, concise and interesting.

I have avoided technical detail in preference to having something "short and sweet" which whets the appetite rather than over indulging it.

I hope that the personal experiences have helped others to identify areas in their own lives where similar things are happening.

It is my earnest wish that I have provided my readers with some guidelines to holistic health and that this will provide them with a stepping stone to peak performance in their lives.

> "To see without sight is **vision**
> To feel without emotion is **love**
> To think without logic is **knowing**
> Nurture all of these and be **whole.**

SUGGESTED FURTHER READING

Book title	Author	Publisher
Anatomy of an Illness	Norman Cousins	Bantam
Aromatherapy, the Essential Beginning	Gary Young	Young
A Doctor's Proven New Home Cure for Arthritis	Giraud W Campbell	Thorsons
A Soul's Journey	Peter Richelieu	Aquarius
Bach Flower Remedies for Women	Judy Howard	Daniel
Bach Flower Remedies, The	John Ramsell	Daniel
Birth Signs	Debbie Frank	Vermilion
Empowerment through Reiki	Paula Horan	Lotus Light
Eva Fraser's Facial Workout	Eva Fraser	Penguin
Family Guide to Alternative Medicine	Reader's Digest	Reader Digest
Family Guide to Homeopathy, The	Dr Andrew Lockie	Simon/Shuster
Fit for Life	Harvey & Marilyn Diamond	Bantam
Flower Essences and Vibrational Healing	Gurudus	Cassandra
Food Combining for Vegetarians	Jackie le Tissier	Thorsons
Guide to Alternative Medicine	Dr Vernon Colman	Corgie
Hands of Light	Barbara Ann Brennan	Bantam
Harmony is the Healer	Ingrid S von Rohr	Element
Heal your Body	Louise Hay	Hay House
Healers on Healing	Carlson & Shield	Perigee
Healing Benefits of Acupressure, The	F C Houston	Keats
Healing with Music and Colour	Mary Bassano	Weiser
Healing Power of Herb Teas, The	Ceres	Thorsons
Health Through God's Pharmacy	Maria Treban	Ennshaler
Herb User's Guide, The	David Hoffman	Thorsons
Herbal Therapy for Women	Elisabeth Brooke	Thorsons
Holistic Aromatherapy	Christine Wildwood	Thorsons
Homeopathic First Aid	Dr Anne Glover	Thorsons
In Tune with the Infinite	Ralph Waldo Trine	Mandala
Joseph Corvo's Zone Therapy	Joseph Corvo	Vermilion
Juicing Detox Diet, The	Caroline Wheater	Thorsons
Lindsey Wagner's New Beauty	Lindsey Wagner	Prentice
Love, Medicine and Miracles	Bernie S Siegel	Arrow
Maria Treban's Cures	Maria Treban	Ennshaler
More Lives than One	Jeffrey Iverson	Pan

Peace, Love and Healing	Bernie Siegal	Rider
Perfect Health	Deepak Chopra	Bantam
Quantum Healing	Deepak Chopra	Bantam
Qi Gong	Dr Effle Chow	Medi Press
Reading the Body	Ohashi	Aquarian
Reflexology and Colour Therapy Workbook, The	Pauline Wills	Element
Reiki - Universal Life Energy	Bodo J Baginski	Life Rhythm
Self Mastery and Fate with the Cycles of Life	H Spencer Lewis	Amorc
Seven Spiritual Laws of Success, The	Deepak Chopra	New World Library
Silica - the Amazing Gel	Klaus Kaufmann	Alive
Spiritual Nutrition and the Rainbow Diet	Gabriel Cousens	Cassandra
Subtle Aromatherapy	Patricia Davis	Daniel
The Therapeutic Touch	Dolores Krieger	Simon / Shuster
Twelve Healers of the Zodiac	Peter Damian	Wieser
Visualisation	Michael Page	Aquarian
The Way of the Wizard	Deepak Chopra	Harmony Books
What Colour are You?	Lilla Bek	Aquarius
You can heal your Life	Louise Hay	Hay House

LIST OF USEFUL ADDRESSES

Rosicrucian Order Amorc
Rosicrucian Park
1342 Naglee Avenue
San Jose
California CA 95191

Rosicrucian Order Amorc
Greenwood Gate
Blackhill
Crowborough
East Sussex TN6 1XE

Personal Biorhythms
10 Middlebrook Road
Bagthorpe
nr. Underwood
Notts. NG16 5H

Robert Haig Coxon Jr.,
RHC Productions
CP/PO Box 4172
Westmount
Quebec H32 3B6
Canada

Gary Young
Young Living Essential Oils
12662 South Redwood Road
Riverton
Utah 84109
USA

The Natural Health Ministry
Well Woman Nutrition Centre
Donegal Town
Co. Donegal
EIRE

Gemstone Remedies
Eldesten Ltd.
NL 3828 Hoogland
Netherlands

Heel Homeopathic Products
Macwils International Trading Ltd.
120 Furness Road
Willesden
London, NW10 5UH

Jeremy Townsend
West of England Aloe Centre
3 Library Lodge
Tetbury
Gloucester, GL8 8DT
Tel. 01666 504 718

Carita House (Leotards)
Stapeley
Nantwich
Cheshire
CW5 7LJ

PREVIOUS PUBLICATIONS
BY THE
SAME AUTHOR

Dance for Gymnastics, Book I (with training cassette)

Dance for Gymnastics, Book II (with training cassette)

Dance Training and Choreography for Gymnasts

The Day I Met Maria (book on cassette)

Magic Meditations for Children - Nature (book on cassette)

The Children are the Guardians of the World (book on cassette)

NEW!

from the Chalice of Trust
The *Third* in the trilogy of talking books by
Jean Honeyman

The Children are the Guardians of the World
This beautiful story brings the knowledge of the dolphins, whales, Aborigines and
Native Americans to the listener, with poetry, prose, music and sound effects. A
deeply moving story for all ages.
On single cassette: only £7.00 UK; £8.00 Europe; £9.00 elsewhere

Also available: Books 1 and 2

Magic meditation for Children
Takes young children on a voyage of discovery into Nature with poetry,
prose, sound effects.
On single cassette: £7.00 UK; £8.00 Europe; £9.00 elsewhere.
The Day I met Maria (Available in German)
Tells the story of an 18 year old girl who is guided through her life's
problems by a beautiful stranger.
On double cassette: £10.00 UK; £11.00 Europe; £12.00 elsewhere

REVIEWS

"Every school library and youth centre should have them"
Kindred Spirit, Autumn 1995
"These tapes are perfect for the spiritual beginner"
On Eagles Wings, Spring 1995
"A ten-minute listen each day should be compulsory."
David Hitchinson, Children's BBC Radio 4

*This trilogy gives simple spiritual information for all ages. These tapes are the
perfect gift for someone special.*

Please send me:

**Payment in sterling only, please
Cheques payable to:
The Chalice of Trust**

_____ copies of "Total Awareness"   = £10.00

_____ copies of "The Children are the Guardians of the World"   = £   .00

_____ copies of "Magic Meditations for Children"   = £   .00

_____ copies of "The Day I met Maria"   = £   .00

_____ copies of "Der Tag, An Dem Ich Maria Traf"   = £   .00

Name _____

Address _____

_____ Tel _____

Send to: The Chalice of Trust, 7 Hothfield Court, Appleby in Westmorland,
Cumbria CA16 6JD Tel. 017683 53016

116 chakras
119 Surgery
120 sound